Wisdom Within

Roger Mills and Elsie Spittle

Authors' Note: Some of the material in this book appeared previously,
in slightly different form, in a self-published volume entitled *The Health
Realization Primer—Empowering Individuals and Communities.*

The Publisher: Lone Pine Publishing

10145 - 81 Avenue	1901 Raymond Ave. SW, Suite C
Edmonton, AB T6E 1W9	Renton, WA 98055
Canada	USA

Website: www.lonepinepublishing.com

Canadian Cataloguing in Publication Data
Mills, Roger C., 1943 –
   The wisdom within

   ISBN 1-55105-288-1

   1. Self-actualization (Psychology) 2. Spirituality—Psychological
aspects. I. Spittle, Elsie B. II. Title.
BF637.S4M556 2001   158.1   C00-911320-7

Editorial Director: Nancy Foulds
Project Editor: Randy Williams
Production Manager: Jody Reekie
Layout & Production: Monica Triska, Arlana Anderson-Hale
Book Design: Heather Markham
Cover Design: Robert Weidemann

We acknowledge the financial support of the Government of Canada
through the Book Publishing Industry Development Program (BPIDP)
for our publishing activities.

PC: P6

TABLE OF CONTENTS

ACKNOWLEDGMENTS

Our deepest appreciation goes to Theosophist and author Sydney Banks. Syd's wisdom has been an inspiration and guiding light. Without his original insight and his steadfast commitment to sharing the three Principles, none of the dramatic results described in this book would have been possible.

Our heartfelt gratitude goes to our spouses for their unwavering love and their dedication to sharing this understanding with others.

Roger Mills and Elsie Spittle

Understanding the Mind—The Route to Mental Stability, Personal Empowerment and Well-being

Rediscovering the Human Spirit

As we enter the new millennium, humanity is at a crossroads. We are seeing runaway technological change, but little improvement in our ability to live satisfying, happy lives. Even with technical sophistication and the pace of change of the material world, we have not had a great deal of success at improving our inner world. Humanity is still beset with prejudice, fear and stress. As a society, we are still debating widely opposing views of how to deal with the pressures of an increasingly hectic life. We don't really understand the causes of behavior that are considered anti-social or "abnormal" in the eyes of society.

People at all levels of social strata, in every culture and lifestyle, are searching for happiness in a wide variety of ways. The methods range from various disciplines of therapy to spin-offs of support groups to widely divergent personal growth practices and spiritual disciplines. Psychology and other academic disciplines that study human nature and behavior compete with politicians, TV commentators, religious leaders and other "gurus" in the debate about what is wrong with society and how we should respond to increasing violence, marital problems, the breakdown of the family, and the crises in our schools and inner cities. After 20 years of nationally funded drug education and prevention programs, drug use and abuse are again on the rise among youth. Professional athletes and entertainers with serious substance abuse and other emotional problems demonstrate that fame and fortune are not the route to guaranteed self-worth or happiness.

This book proposes a solution to these problems and more. It is based on new discoveries about human nature, about how we tick as human beings at a very fundamental level. These discoveries reveal some fascinating things about how the Mind works to produce the way each human being sees and experiences life, day in and day out. These discoveries are hopeful and inspiring. They possess the magical power to transform our inner reality in much the same way that harnessing the power of electricity allowed us to transform our level of physical comfort and ease.

The first discovery is that everyone has access to an understanding of the Universal Principles that create the human experience of life. Secondly, when people become aware of these Principles in action in their day to day lives, they find a new frame of reference, one composed of deeper wisdom, better judgment and more happiness.

> **"Mind, Consciousness and Thought are the three**
> **Principles that enable us to acknowledge and respond**
> **to existence."**
> —Sydney Banks, *The Missing Link*, p. 21

Mind is the life-force behind all things, the formless energy and intelligence of life itself. Mind operates before the form of our personal reality. *Consciousness* is the ability to be aware of reality and to recognize how reality is created. *Thought* is the power to think and thereby create our personal experience of reality. Mind, Consciousness and Thought are the links between the formless and the unique reality each of us perceives as an individual.

The words Mind, Consciousness and Thought may evoke in the reader associations with esoteric spiritual or "new age" personal growth practices. The terms are not meant in that way in this book. They are meant to describe universal scientific principles, similar to a principle like gravity or electromagnetism; these principles of physics operate continuously to affect our movements and the relationships between physical objects. These laws are invisible but are always operating. The three Principles—Mind, Consciousness and Thought—are always operating as well. While they may be invisible, the way they work together at every moment determines the form each person's reality takes. The goal of this book is to demystify the operation of these Principles in everyday life.

One of the discoveries that has surprised the authors, in a wonderful way, is that ordinary people from all walks of life can begin to see the operation of these Principles in their daily lives. They are then able to use this understanding in very practical ways to dramatically improve the quality of their lives. Many people say that once the logic connects with them, they see it as basic common sense. Their feel for how the Principles create their everyday realities grows naturally from there.

In this book, the authors will use Mind, with a capital "M", to point to or describe the operation of this Principle. The word mind, with a lower case "m," here means our individual, personal minds—including the brain and the thoughts stored there. Consciousness, with a capital "C," refers to the Principle of Consciousness, while consciousness (lower case "c") refers to personal consciousness. Thought, with a capital "T," refers to the Principle of Thought. This version is used, for example, to describe or point to the role of Thought. The use of "thought," with a lower case "t," refers to our personal thinking. This form is used when describing the content of everyone's individual reality.

This book will also use the words "insight" and "realization" to describe a shift to a deeper level of understanding about how reality is created from inside out. Insights come from innate wisdom. Wisdom is the capacity that shows us how to live a more flowing and productive, less stressful life—irrespective of where we are now.

What These Discoveries Offer

These discoveries clarify some new knowledge about the human spirit and the depth of our capacity for happiness, insight and wisdom. Like electricity, this knowledge has been around since the beginning of time, but only now has it been uncovered to the point where it can be put into use in everyday life. This knowledge is evident in many native or indigenous tribes' spiritual teachings and in every major mystical school of philosophy. It is described in small bits and pieces by some schools of psychology. It is buried beneath the rituals and techniques of many personal growth movements. The problem is that it is so well hidden that it is made to seem ephemeral, too esoteric and unrealistic for most to attain. This kind of understanding is often attached to a maze of differing lifestyles, personalities, "shoulds" and rituals or stringent self-denial practices.

The Difficulty of Explaining Wisdom

When the authors first learned about these Principles, they themselves did not understand what the Principles had to do with their daily lives or with facing their problems, stress and frustrations. Yet merely uncovering the existence of these underlying forces was enough to trigger a completely natural, effortless and self-generating process of change. Healthy, liberating changes in the authors' thinking and in views of life kept happening almost in spite of them.

To understand these Principles, one needs only to realize how experience is generated. The process can be best understood if it is broken down into three truths: 1) Experience is generated from inside out—continuously—via the operation of the three Principles of Mind, Consciousness and Thought; 2) Anyone has the ability to think and interpret life with free will; and 3) Thought is the force that creates everyone's personal picture of life; once this process is understood, a person's outlook begins to change automatically. We do not have to adopt self-improvement rituals or practices trying to think more positive thoughts. We don't need to analyze or figure out our thinking. With the realization of one simple fact about where experiences originate—in ourselves—

positive change can begin. This amazingly simple recognition triggers everything else.

What the authors are aiming for with this book is to give the reader an understanding so simple that it can't be explained. The authors are seeking to facilitate a change in the reader's level of consciousness. Because this change is not related to the intellect, it is impossible to explain levels of consciousness in an intellectual way. When any person's level of consciousness rises, he or she becomes more conscious of the operation of the Principles behind reality. This book will attempt to help the reader by 1) describing the logic of the Principles and their consequences; 2) describing how the Principles demonstrate their existence in our daily lives; and 3) providing examples of how individuals or groups have found an easier, more effective route to desired changes via their understanding of these Principles.

Unlike intellectual learning or analysis, there is no way of predicting when an insight or realization about the Principles will occur. The authors cannot presume to tell people what to do to get these insights. To do so would run the risk of putting negative thoughts into readers' heads if they began to worry about whether they were doing these things right, doing them often enough, or whether the techniques used shouldn't be producing more dramatic results. We can only prepare for insight by pointing ourselves toward a sincere appreciation for the gift of Thought, and toward "Seeing" the operation of these Principles in our own lives every day.

Faith and hope are also powerful pulls toward understanding. The authors have seen people change dramatically merely because they began to trust that they had something more pure and beautiful inside them and that they were already wise, healthy people. Thus, when you read stories or examples in this book, look at these stories as *your* story. We all function the same way, using the same Principles. Trusting the existence of wisdom will produce change, because that trust enables us to question the reality of our learned, insecure thoughts.

The authors have found that this understanding can be shared in a wide variety of settings, from public housing projects to police officer training programs to the corporate sector. It can be shared in a respectful, common-sense manner that allows people to be ordinary, to be themselves and to find something natural and beautiful in themselves and in life. All that is required is a simple understanding of how the Mind works to produce reality via Thought and Consciousness.

The Power of This Understanding

This understanding has been applied for more than 20 years with exciting, inspiring and highly promising outcomes in clinical applications, in prevention and early intervention programs, and in widespread, comprehensive community empowerment projects with disadvantaged, at-risk populations. It has been applied toward improving quality of work life and leadership programs in multinational corporations. By studying the outcomes of these programs, we can now have a better understanding of how people lose their bearings and question their mental health, their ability to enjoy life and to use common sense. We can also have a better understanding of the root cause of emotional disturbances and of how to help people live satisfying, self-sufficient and healthy lives. Even more, these discoveries can point anyone in the direction of living his or her ideal life with joy and magic, happiness and success, far beyond what he or she had previously considered possible.

How Did These Discoveries Come About?

During the 1970s Dr. Mills was primary investigator at the University of Oregon for a National Institute of Mental Health research-demonstration grant on preventing mental illness and reducing the number of individuals with chronic dependency on either mental health or social services. His first position after completing graduate school had been as executive director of Oregon's first federally funded community mental health center. As a young professional fresh out of an innovative, multidisciplinary doctoral program at the University of Michigan, he was eager to apply his academic knowledge to make a difference in the world. As he and other researchers examined the programs and patterns of patient flow through Oregon's community mental health system, they were alarmed at the extremely high rates of relapse and chronicity. They found that these same statistics held true nationally. The Mental Health Center's ex-hospital program, for example, had as a program objective to reduce recidivism from 85 to 80% for their clients. Data on patient flow indicated that many clients would come into detox for drug and alcohol problems, go through in patient, group home and outpatient treatment, then be on their own for only a short while before they ended up back in the hospital or detox center for another journey through the system. Stress problems seemed chronic and without end.

As an adjunct faculty member at the University of Oregon, Dr. Mills worked with his colleagues on a grant for funding to examine what would genuinely work to enable people to become more self-sufficient. According to Dr. Mills, "We wanted to conduct research on what factors enable people to live a life of personal satisfaction with the ability to solve their own problems. From my position as director of a center staffed by psychiatrists, psychologists and other therapists, I felt their almost continual frustrations and stress. One senior staff member told me that new therapists were routinely told not to give their clients too much hope because clients normally did not get much better. Because we did not understand how to provide clients with a solid sense of well-being and stability, it was hard for professionals to reach those goals for themselves. Many were suffering stress to the point where their marriages were failing, their relationships with co-workers were upsetting and conflict-based, and they were unhappy in their work. When we surveyed these professionals to find out what they wanted in terms of continuing education programs, most requests were in the areas of stress and burnout."

The five-year research-demonstration programs enabled Dr. Mills and his team to look both inside and outside the mainstream approaches in the field: "We were willing to try anything that had a reasonable, ethical and common-sense foundation of logic that seemed promising. We brought in some programs that taught people how beliefs, attitudes and biases learned from prior experiences affected their outlook and subsequently their behavior. We observed more improvement in the participants of this program, known as the Good Neighbor Project, than with the other 28 pilot programs concurrently being done around the state. However, the changes were not substantially beyond results claimed by other personal growth seminars and methods."

A Deeper Understanding of the Mind

In 1974 Dr. Mills heard from psychologists in Canada that a layperson without formal professional training had realized something very profound about the nature of Mind, and behavior's link to the way the Mind works by using Thought and Consciousness. He also heard that people listening to the wisdom of this man, Sydney Banks, were undergoing substantial, almost miraculous changes in the quality of their lives. While skeptical, he and his colleagues were also curious. Dr. Mills recalls:

> "In early 1975 I went to the island in British Columbia where Syd Banks resided, feeling anxious about the nature of my trip, but also excited about the possibility of finding something that would add a new dimension to our understanding of Thought.

> "What I ran into there was something beyond anything I had dreamed would occur in my lifetime. Prior to hearing Sydney Banks, I was able to meet and talk with several couples and individuals who had regularly attended his lectures. They immediately struck me as genuinely happy, stable and self-assured. They were not eager to promote what they had found, nor were they proselytizing or 'groupie.' Yet they could describe what they had learned about Thought in a logically compelling and inspiring way that connected with their daily life experiences. They were consistently down to earth, humorous and insightful. They seemed to have a genuine respect, caring and compassion for everyone, and they were productive and successful in their own careers. As I got to know these people better, I followed their lives over time. I recognized that, by any standards, they exhibited a sustained

level of mental health, wisdom, grace and maturity that was above the norm of society. Elsie Spittle and her husband, Ken, were one of the couples who greatly impressed me with the depth of their wisdom and their loving, compassionate stance toward others, myself included.

"As a researcher, I was interested in the history of these families. I found that most had survived an extremely negative past. Some had been psychiatric patients, some on the verge of divorce; others had been addicted to either illegal or prescription drugs or had problems with alcohol. Some had been on public assistance, living at a subsistence level for most of their prior adult lives. Some had dropped out of society because they had not been able to handle the stress of work or career demands. Yet now they did not seem to show any adverse effects of the hardships or early childhood traumas that had affected them earlier. They were able to put their own past in perspective. They now recognized their old habits of thinking with such neutrality that they were able to lead productive, rewarding lives without acting as if they were anything special.

"When I first listened to Sydney Banks describe the nature of Mind and the role of Thought and Consciousness, I was disturbed because he was so very matter of fact about his discoveries. He seemed absolutely certain that everyone has a direct connection, via Thought, to a more profound intelligence and higher order feelings of love and understanding. Many of his observations flew in the face of everything I had learned in graduate school or in my post-graduate work. He seemed equally certain that there was a cure or an answer for every condition. This conclusion was certainly very different from what I had learned both during my training and in my experience in the field of psychology. Yet the more I came to know those who had learned something from Sydney Banks's talks, the more impressed I was by the profound nature of the change in these individuals. The fact that Syd's experience happened without premeditation or forethought was astounding to me, as was the depth of his realization about Mind and human nature."

Ordinary Lives and Profound Wisdom

Dr. Mills brought other researchers and psychologists to the island, and they were all impressed by the people they met, by their lack of therapeutic ritual or interest in any personal growth technique or method. These laypeople were very ordinary in how they conducted their lives, yet they exhibited a profound wisdom and presence. The professionals, however, were disturbed that there was no technique or "textbook method" that they could adopt for use with their clients. In fact, Syd kept saying that *all* techniques merely produce a placebo effect and perpetuate the illusion that something outside of ourselves has produced a result.

Still, Dr. Mills and his colleagues could not deny that they themselves were changing and seeing life differently. According to Dr. Mills, "Even as I remained skeptical and confused, I began to change. I noticed that I was feeling quieter inside and taking things more in stride. The idea that Thought is the most basic building block of reality at every moment in our lives was foreign to me, given all of my prior training. As with most people, I experienced life coming at me from outside in. My emotions, my behavior, the quality of my thinking, my stress and my inner life all seemed like understandable reactions to my past and current situation. The role of Thought in this process was invisible as any kind of independent variable. As my mind quieted down, some of my insecure thoughts, expectations and habits of judgment seemed less important to me."

At some point, the function of Thought started to become more visible to these practitioners. One therapist stated: "As my mind slowed down, I could notice the thoughts that came into my head. They did not seem as compelling as they had before. I gained a little distance from their iron grip. I could also see that if I made these thoughts important they would result in feelings of resentment, self-righteousness, anger or self-pity. Seeing Thought as leading to emotions that kept me in the grip of a certain way of perceiving things was extremely freeing. It led to reduced stress and a bigger picture perspective with a deeper clarity about what was actually happening."

The Impact on the Authors' Lives and Work

Elsie Spittle clearly recalls the day she first met Roger Mills:

"Sydney Banks had invited Ken and me to meet two psychologists who were about to call on Sydney Banks. We were the first ones to arrive and had just made ourselves comfortable when Syd called out, 'Here they are.' We trooped out to the kitchen to welcome the visitors. Coming down the driveway on crutches was a large, red-haired man who had his foot in a cast. The man accompanying him had his arm in a sling. I had not met many psychologists, but I was expecting them to be in a suit and tie and more serious in appearance. Instead they were casually dressed and, despite their injuries, seemed in good spirits. Although they didn't look like I imagined, I immediately became interested in the conversation they began with Syd. It was apparent that they were fascinated by what Syd was saying but at the same time I could see disbelief registering on their faces as he clearly and confidently described his philosophy. I understood that reaction as I had experienced the same thing earlier for a period of almost two years. Ken and I had known Syd prior to his profound discovery about the nature of Mind, and we initially found it extremely difficult to accept the incredible change that occurred in Syd. That a man with minimal education and no psychological training could have an insight so transcendent that he could describe the relationship between Mind, Consciousness and Thought with absolute certainty was beyond our understanding. I became quite indignant whenever he would make such statements—I had no idea that this discovery had anything of value to offer the world.

"It was very difficult for me to grasp the idea that my experience of life had something to do with my thinking. I thought our experiences were generated by external events and that we merely reacted to them to the best of our ability. My thinking was very closed off to a deeper understanding on how the three Principles work together to create reality. I believed that I had no part in the process, that I was a victim of my circumstances. That belief gave me a lot of latitude to berate my husband and children, and to complain about my perceived inability to move ahead in life.

"However, once I began to understand the role of Thought and discovered how deeper feelings guide us toward mental health, I became a different person. I saw my family with new eyes, with much more understanding and compassion. My family, friends and colleagues noticed a change in me, telling me that I was calmer and easier to be around, not so critical and judgmental. A whole new world opened up for me—it was like magic. Opportunities to share what I was learning presented themselves. Soon I was traveling around the country and training others. Never did I dream this would be possible with my limited education and financial resources. Yet it *was* happening, almost in spite of myself.

"Roger Mills was among the first psychologists who came to training sessions that I occasionally had the privilege of conducting with Syd. Roger introduced me to many of his colleagues and arranged for me to do seminars around the country. Over the years Roger and I have continued to work together at various times.

"In 1984, I moved with my husband and daughter to Miami to work with a group of professionals who had started a clinic and educational institute. I was also conducting leadership development programs for the corporate sector in other parts of Florida. In 1986 we moved to Tampa, where I helped set up another educational center that offered programs to corporations and mental health professionals. In 1988 I was introduced to residents from a community housing project that Roger Mills had begun in 1987 at the Modello Public Housing Community in Miami. I was so impressed and moved by the stories of change that the residents related that I began to focus on developing a community project in Tampa.

"In 1996, Ken and I moved to Los Angeles, where Roger and I founded a consulting and training institute and worked together for the next four years. Both Ken and I have the highest regard and deep appreciation for the contributions Roger has made to the field of psychology and to society."

For Roger Mills, exposure to the three Principles would lead to a profound change in the direction of his life and his career. Dr. Mills recalls:

"The way that my own life began to change following this initial exposure was tantamount to being pulled into a whole new world. One of the first things I recognized was that the insights or realizations that genuinely contributed to happiness and peace of mind had nothing to do with my past or with any intellectual 'figuring out.' In fact they were much more likely to occur when my intellect—of which I had always been proud—was quiet, when I literally had nothing on my mind. My intellect, the source of all of my ideas about my own self-image and self-worth, was thrown for a loop. At times I strenuously resisted the simple but elegant logic behind these findings, yet I could see their potential for unifying many different schools of thought and philosophies. Seen from the historical perspective of all we have learned in psychology, I realized that these insights could provide a more scientific basis for understanding both the mind and human nature at a more basic level. They also provided an understanding that helped people grow to a new level of maturity that was natural, genuine and sustained. Yet the process by which people were changing was very different than the ways I had been trained to think about what it takes to create sustained change.

"Colleagues who were being exposed to these insights were reporting similar changes. The refreshing depth of wisdom and self-assurance exhibited by the people I had met in Canada was also beginning to emerge in our clients in Oregon and California. I felt incredibly lucky to have stumbled onto something so unique and profound that demonstrated the ability to help people to this extent. I started to realize that we had vastly underestimated the profound power of the Principles in creating experience as well as the innate capacity for mental health in all people."

In the remainder of this book, the authors will describe these discoveries and demonstrate how they have led to vastly improved levels of well-being in people from all walks of life. Inspiring results have been achieved, even in those who had been written off as incurable or chronic. These discoveries can also help you, the reader, discover new levels of serenity, satisfaction and success in this fascinating journey called life.

INTRODUCTION

Living a Life of Success, Serenity and Satisfaction

New Possibilities for Change

Beginning in 1987, Dr. Mills received funding from the U.S. Departments of Justice and Housing & Urban Development to take the initial findings about the Principles (summarized in the Preface) into pilot programs with inner city schools and neighborhoods. In the course of these programs, Roger worked with substance abuse treatment and prevention programs, community colleges, youth programs, public schools, job training programs, state and county family service agencies and the public housing authority. In 1990 these initial programs received national media attention for their promising outcomes. Subsequently, these kinds of projects spread throughout the United States and abroad. The discoveries described in this book are increasingly being applied in residential treatment for drug and alcohol problems, in educational curricula from elementary through high school, in corporate leadership and employee empowerment programs, in community organizing and development, in outpatient individual and group therapy, in stress management and human relations courses and in psychology courses at universities.

These pilot programs, clinical work and widespread community initiatives led to a fascinating and wonderful discovery. People can, and do, change much more easily than was previously recognized. These changes lead to a higher quality of life that becomes permanent. We all have a natural mechanism for positive change that is "hard-wired" into us. This mechanism involves a simple understanding of the three Principles behind life experience. People who had insights into how these Principles operate in their lives changed beyond what anyone had thought possible. This understanding is natural, innate and very ordinary.

Grasping the operation of these Principles in action and seeing how they work together makes change simple and natural for people who have been exposed to these discoveries. These results in turn led to the discovery that there is a much deeper wellspring of mental stability, happiness and wisdom directly available to us. This wisdom comes to us via a natural process. The authors have seen this inborn resource, or capacity, emerge in people from all walks of life. They have observed this inner resource providing hope and new insights that allowed people to make huge leaps in their lives, from being drug-addicted welfare mothers in public housing to being health professionals who own their own homes; from being stressed executives turning to drugs or alcohol for fear of losing their jobs, homes or families, to being stable, wise and visionary leaders who thrive on their work and truly appreciate the joys of family life.

The authors have conducted programs in communities ranging from upper middle class families of business executives to communities in the most hardcore, poverty- and crime-stricken neighborhoods imaginable. They have seen this wellspring of health emerge in people from all of these situations. Nationally acclaimed results have been achieved in programs in jails, in court-mandated schools for delinquent youth, in public housing and with professionals and mental health practitioners who themselves were burned-out, anxious and depressed. The authors have seen couples go from tolerating each other for the sake of the children to falling deeply in love again; they have also seen people whose lives were riddled with anxiety, fear, doubt and anger become wise, happy and caring, with no doubts about their ability to live a fulfilling life.

What Has Been Discovered About Wisdom?

Daniel Goleman, author of the best-selling book *Emotional Intelligence*, has argued that there is a different kind of intelligence—an EQ as opposed to IQ—that enables people to enjoy life, exercise good judgment, and be sane, happy, well-adjusted people. Goleman suspected there might be things that could be done to nurture or strengthen this emotional intelligence (EQ), yet he was not sure where it originated or how it worked. He also felt that it varied from person to person and that some of us have more of this intelligence than others. He suggested methods for people to gain more of this type of intelligence.

The authors have found, in repeated clinical trials and community applications with a variety of groups over a 20-year span, that every person has this "emotional intelligence" at their disposal, everyday, if they *know where it originates and how to access this capacity*. The key to helping both clients and colleagues unleash this intelligence in themselves has consistently been: 1) To provide a better, practical understanding of how Mind, Consciousness and Thought work together to generate everyone's perception of reality; 2) To show that they already have this wiser mode of thought within them; 3) To describe how they can recognize the experience when it emerges; and 4) To help them understand how this wisdom gets buried and why it sometimes seems unimaginable that it can be found again.

After years of applications and follow-up work with people from every imaginable culture, lifestyle, income and education level, the authors have concluded that this deeper intelligence doesn't come from anything we learn in school. It comes from within the depths of our own souls—from the *psyche*. It comes from a natural state of mind that is in us *before* our personalities or cultures and our problems begin. When people discover their capacity for this intelligence, they are able to apply it to their unique and personal situation in life.

Why This Intelligence Appears Elusive

The only reason this emotional intelligence, or wisdom, seems elusive is that we have been looking for it in the wrong places. We don't recognize how our thinking works to give importance or meaning to things outside us. Thus, we get attached to habits of thinking that are a poor substitute for this intelligence. This poorer substitute entails, at best, myriad efforts at coping with and managing stress as the *best we think we can do*. The understanding this book will be pointing to doesn't come to us from our personal thinking or from anything we have read, heard or studied. It comes as realizations from *an inner source of wisdom* beneath our own previously held ideas, beliefs and intellectual concepts.

Sometimes this understanding shows itself as common sense, sometimes as a complete shift in perspective about an event or circumstance, and sometimes as a discovery of some aspect of life or the world we hadn't seen before. These realizations come from a state of purer thinking and responding inside our own consciousness, a psychological space that is the source of a less personal thought process. People use it without even knowing they are doing so because it seems so natural and ordinary at the time. It just seems as if we clearly see what we need to do in an instinctive and obvious way. Some people refer to it as being "on a roll," being "in the flow" or "in the zone" (the authors will tie the three Principles to that "zone" in Chapter Six). We all have a profound understanding of life built in to us, but we often fail to use it or even to recognize we possess it.

Mental Health: More Than Reduction of Symptoms or Problems

What surprised the authors more than anything was the extent of the changes found when they conducted follow-up studies with clients who had learned about this intelligence. The clients had all become very wise, mature and stable people who loved their lives; they brought creativity, innovation and high-quality feelings of enthusiasm and satisfaction to their work. These clients didn't take things personally or look down on others who were unhappy or hard to get along with. They took responsibility for their own feelings and behavior in a natural and dignified way. They treated others with respect and consideration. Their understanding let them become their own teachers.

These people were not only mentally healthy, but they also knew where their mental health originated and how to bring it back. They could quickly get themselves back on track after becoming caught up in negative emotional states. One woman, who had suffered through years of chronic depression and reliance on antidepressants, noticed that when she began to feel happy it scared her, as she had come to believe her happiness couldn't last. "I had been taught that my default setting was depression, and it seemed that way for years," she said. "Now I recognize that the opposite is true; life for me now is fresh, humorous and fun most of the time." People who were chronic worriers or suffered different types of anxiety and paranoid disorders saw that these thoughts were merely learned habits, ways of coping that they had considered normal or necessary. With an appreciation for their innate intelligence, they replaced these habits with a state of mental clarity and common sense. This new perspective allowed them to master life's trials and tribulations without chronic worry, fear or panic.

The authors' findings, gathered from across a wide spectrum of people, led to the conclusion that: Mental health is much more than reducing emotional suffering or eliminating symptoms of distress.

Life is designed to be lived in a way that is much more than coping or merely trying to stay "on top of things."

Just as any human being can live in a great deal of emotional pain, anyone can experience deep feelings of well-being.

A Fresh Look at Human Nature

These results, duplicated with people from all walks of life, represent a new and extraordinarily hopeful set of facts about human nature. These findings have caused countless professionals in psychology, in human services and the helping fields to take a fresh look at the depth and nature of the human potential.

What they are learning brings our vision of this potential from the ethereal to the practical.

When we start to see that there is something deeper already inside us, we can easily go beyond the goal of reducing dissatisfaction in our lives. When we experience more well-being and peace of mind, we find relief from merely trying to alleviate suffering. We start to move into real mental health. As will be shown in more depth in Chapter Seven, real mental health means joyously thriving on life. Although we may periodically slip into coping and feeling overwhelmed or distressed, these states of mind become the exception rather than the rule. Their infrequent occurrence makes us more grateful for how much we have changed and for how we now live. We are no longer left wishing we could find relief from the adverse effects of our pasts, from bad habits or from our ingrained, self-destructive ways of thinking.

Wisdom as a Natural Mode of Thought

Chapter One will describe in more depth the three Principles that are always functioning behind everyday reality, and will explore how the Principles work together to create all the varied and unique versions of reality that humans experience across the globe.

Chapter Two will show how an understanding of these Principles allows the deeper clearer "emotional intelligence"—what this book refers to as wisdom—to emerge. The chapter will describe the source of our deeper intelligence and will explore what wisdom looks like and how it is experienced. Lastly, the chapter will show how wisdom emerges naturally in the process of something we do, literally, all the time—think. Chapter Three will describe the role of feelings and emotions as products of Thought. In this chapter, the reader will learn how feelings and emotions act as an accurate guide to let us know, immediately, whether we are moving toward mental health and wisdom or away from these inborn attributes toward becoming an unwitting prisoner of our personal, insecure thinking.

Chapter Four will explore the ways in which insecure thinking blocks access to wisdom. This chapter will attempt to show how insecure habits of thinking are really a smokescreen that evaporates on its own if one has an understanding of the three Principles. Chapter Five will explore more fully the practical benefits of grasping the Principles as articulated in Chapter One. Chapter Six will explore the implications of these findings for living and functioning more naturally in the "zone," or natural flow of life, that comes with our deeper wisdom. Chapter Seven will try to demonstrate how this understanding brings our birthright of mental health alive, in a very natural and spontaneous way, without the need to continually strive, work on ourselves or adopt therapeutic rituals.

Chapter Eight will revisit in more depth how understanding in and of itself leads to change. Chapter Nine will offer some practical guidelines for staying pointed in the right direction toward deeper levels of wisdom. Chapter Ten will explore how the Principles work in relationships—a very fertile area of life—and will reveal more about the nature of separate realties. The final chapter will explore how these Principles can help society as a whole.

The authors hope that by the time you reach the end of this book, you will appreciate the depth of mental health and wisdom you already have within you. The book

should help you to recognize how these Principles operate both to provide access to wisdom and to take us away
from it. Further, it should help you to understand why
we get gripped by thinking about ourselves, about events
in our lives, about circumstances that trouble us. The
authors will describe the source of a wiser mode of
thought that can contribute to making things better and
will explain how this understanding empowers people
to choose their own outlook and not be adversely
affected by outside circumstances.

This understanding itself is the catalyst for change.
Things can always get better when we see our lives
through the perspective of wisdom. An understanding of
the Principles outlined in this book will help you see
through any situation to the real truth of the matter, to
know with certainty and confidence that you are in control and have the sense to know what is needed, with no
feelings of worry, confusion or alienation.

Seeing Past Our Current Outlook

These findings provide a new look at the power
behind our ideas about reality. Our ideas about life,
our points of view and our beliefs do not so much
reflect reality as determine it for each of us. The logic
presented in this book reveals a deeper dimension of
reality. These findings illustrate how the Principles, as
universal common denominators, are subtly but
surely behind how we experience any event or circumstance in our lives. These Principles have not yet
been widely recognized within the field of psychology.
Or, if acknowledged, they have been relegated to the
realm of religion and philosophy. As stated earlier, the
authors found the Principles to be *completely natural*
and consistently available in a very practical, down-
to-earth way.

Recently, a woman attending a 10-week resident empow-erment class in a program based on the three Principles stated that she had suddenly realized one day that she was in a destructive cycle with her husband. She was working while he was unemployed. To mask his insecure feelings about not being a good provider, he would stay out late at night, drinking with his buddies and coming home at 3:00 or 4:00 in the morning. She would usually stay up, wait on the stairs and give him hell when he arrived. As a result of learning about the Principles in class, she saw how her behavior was perceived by him in a way that made him all the more insecure and guilty, and thus more likely to stay out all night the next night as well. She saw that she didn't need to react to his behavior.

The woman stated that it just came to her as common sense that what she had been doing in her upset state of mind wasn't helping her husband or herself. So she started just going to bed and getting a good night's sleep. She would be loving, affectionate and compas-sionate in the morning, and he couldn't figure out at first why she wasn't reacting when he tried to provoke her. After a few weeks he began coming home earlier because he enjoyed her new feelings toward him. He later asked about getting into the empowerment class himself. He started to attend classes and enrolled in a union-sponsored carpentry apprentice program at the same time.

The purpose of this book is to help people, like this couple, in all walks of life find a happier, more fulfill-ing, stress-free life. The tricky part is that the authors will be describing something that all of us already have, but most of us don't realize we have! Thus, in order to be helped, we must see a deeper psychological fact about ourselves directly: We must see through the maze of distortions and biases, the mental fog created by our learned ideas and concepts.

The good news is that these facts are very simple and obvious once they are seen. They resonate with common sense, with our intuitive appreciation for life as a universal human experience before the different roles, personalities and positions everyone takes on. The idea is to take a look "behind the screen," to see how each individual's personal picture of life is formed and projected in the first place. With a clear grasp of these facts, we can move toward life becoming more like "heaven on earth."

How to Approach This Material

The authors are hopeful that you are open to reading this book differently than you would other self-help or self-improvement books. Often when people read these kinds of books, they look for a technique or a "cookie-cutter" set of steps they can follow. They are asking what they can do, what they can try or strive toward to have a better, more satisfying, stress-free life. The discoveries behind this book show that there is nothing that we need to do in terms of learning "life skills" or trying our best to practice behaviors or activities designed to produce change. These behaviors or therapeutic rituals, in most instances, only substitute one source of insecure or self-conscious thinking for another. In fact there is nothing at all outside of us that can provide lasting help that doesn't result in *that thing itself* becoming another source of dependency.

For example, meditation can be a wonderful, calming, relaxing feeling—but if you *try* to meditate when you are stressed and things are hectic, *trying* to meditate will often add another level of stress. Another example would be trying to substitute a positive thought for a negative one, often referred to as "positive thinking." With this approach, if you are really gripped by the negative thought, *trying* to replace it with a positive thought adds stress. With natural wisdom, simply understanding that stress is created by how we think about certain situations is enough to release the stress and pressure that we are experiencing. We then automatically move into a state of calm and quiet.

What we want to be able to do is to understand how our minds are using thought to continuously determine personal reality at each moment. Whether this view of reality is wise or foolish, it is created in the same manner—by our thinking at the time. Can we grasp how this process works enough to distinguish wisdom from arbitrary rigid habits of thinking? The authors have found that answer to be yes.

Rather than telling you to do anything, what this book aims at is the recognition of these simple Principles. These Principles have to be seen directly or "realized"; they cannot be understood intellectually. If this understanding is to have any real benefit for you, grasping it with the intellect is not the way to proceed. This book will present Principles, and offer real life examples of these Principles. It will attempt to clarify how one consistent logic explains things we have all experienced in relationships, in our struggles with stress or low moods, and in our concerns about how the past seems to be affecting us now. The idea is to read between the lines, beyond the details of each story or analogy, to see and *feel* the facts of the matter. Once the Principles come alive for us, we are on our way to a better life.

Taking a Less Personal Stance Toward Our Thinking

In pilot programs, the authors found that the best way to teach and to learn about these discoveries is impersonally, in the way we would study math or any other science. One of the reasons we, as a society, have gone off track in understanding human nature is that we have taken our personal thinking much too seriously. We have tried to find greater meaning and significance in our individual differences or separate realities. We look in our personal world of "needs," desires or insecurity to find better relationships, more fulfillment or happiness. The answer to our search cannot be found in this way. In fact it is only our personal thoughts that keep us from the answer.

The answer is quite simple. It exists as a consistent, and fascinating, common denominator—something that is as constant as gravity in that it has a predictable impact for everyone's psychological makeup. This common denominator is the manner in which each of us uses these Principles in everyday life. Understanding the role of Thought, as both the *transmitter and fabric* of everyone's reality, immediately takes us to a deeper dimension of wisdom. The following chapter describes in more detail the way that the three Principles of Mind, Consciousness and Thought work in relation to our thinking, emotions and behavior.

CHAPTER ONE

The Three Principles Behind Our Moment-to-Moment Experience of Life

Every field of study looks for deeper underlying principles. Discovery of deeper principles makes that field simpler because more of the events or things being studied can be explained with a common, overarching logic. When Einstein, for example, found a common link between energy and matter, he could state that link with a simple equation ($E = MC^2$). Understanding this relationship solved a whole range of problems in the field of physics. The authors would assert that the three Principles described in this chapter, and their relationship to one another, explain the common link to the underlying pattern or logic of the entire spectrum of human behavior.

The authors have found, in practice, that every human behavior can be derived from this logic. Just as the principle of gravity affects everyone on earth in the same way, at all times, the Principles presented here explain every kind of human psychological experience. Every feeling, emotion, culture and behavior across the globe can be explained within the framework provided by three Principles: Mind, Consciousness and Thought.

Grasping the logic of these Principles is the first step to being able to use this understanding in your own life, in your work and in your community. As you read this chapter, look for the ways this logic applies in very practical ways to your everyday behavior.

The first thing that the logic of these Principles makes clear is why our thinking appears to be so real to each of us. It helps us understand how we tick—how our mental processes work at each moment to determine how life looks. It explains why life looks different to each one of us. It helps us see, in a practical way: 1) When to rely on our prior learning and memories for useful information; 2) when not to rely on beliefs or expectations from the past; and 3) how to access our wiser thinking. It explains why we move back and forth from "common sense" to feeling confused, stressed and anxious. It shows how all of these feelings stem from insecure, *conditioned* thinking. It clarifies why we sometimes feel on top of the world and sometimes buried underneath it. It puts us in charge of our own thinking and behavior by providing a deeper understanding of the nature of life as a human experience.

The Principles that determine each person's experience of life are Mind, Consciousness and Thought. Thought, before the form of each person's thinking, is the ability to create images in our heads. It is our individual power, yet it is a power that is universal, one which allows us to produce and experience any reality we want. Mind, Consciousness and Thought work together to make our thinking appear real. These Principles work in unison from inside out to create our reality. They are always at work within us, whether we are aware of it or not.

The Principle of Mind

Mind is the purest life force, the source of power *behind life itself.* It is a formless energy and a universal intelligence that provides the ability for all human beings to think about and to experience their lives. Mind, Consciousness and Thought combine to produce the form our reality takes. Just as electricity is the power source that turns on our lights and appliances, *Mind, Consciousness and Thought work before form,* enabling us to create our reality. Thus reality is always, at each moment in time, being created, formed and reformed from the inside out.

It is impossible to provide an easy-to-grasp description of what Mind does because Mind is the source of all description. It creates and generates our picture of reality according to how we think about things. It operates behind the scenes, *before the form, before the specific contents of our thinking.* Therefore, it is impossible to have any intellectual picture or accurate model of Mind because that model is itself a product *of* Mind.

Yet we experience the workings of Mind continually. What we access when we step back from our personal thinking is the power—the impersonal, universal intelligence that is Mind. Everyone can experience the pure intelligence behind his or her thinking. We experience this deep intelligence as insights or what people might call "a-ha" moments. These realizations give us a clearer, more objective and wiser view of things—a view that cannot be accessed via our personal thinking.

While Mind as a universal intelligence does not tell us what or how to think, it does make our thinking take on the appearance of reality, whether this thinking is in the form of our innate wisdom or in the form of our personal thinking.

Mind is not the same thing as the brain. The brain is a biological computer and a transmitter. It merely stores and transmits thought content (specific ideas, values, beliefs or insights). Similarly, electricity is a force in nature. It does not originate in the wiring in our homes, or in our computers or our batteries—it exists first as a formless energy. The flow of this energy follows certain laws or principles that, once understood, allow us to harness and make use of its power. In fact, the newest research in physics has led scientists to discover that every kind of matter begins as pure, formless energy that is transmuted into form.

Mind is a formless energy and a Universal Intelligence before the form of the body or the brain. The three Principles govern how this energy is converted into the unique reality that each individual human being experiences. The Principles are the laws that govern this transformation. While these laws may be *described* intellectually, they cannot be truly *understood* in that manner—they must be realized and recognized via insight.

Once any person begins to realize—by means of an insight—how the three Principles work, that person can reshape his or her reality. Rather than accepting that the world is fixed and intractable, people can actually change their perspective at a very fundamental level if they so choose. An analogy would be the artist who makes pottery from clay. While the clay is soft, the artist shapes it into a vase or bowl. When the clay hardens, it seems as if it was never soft and formless, but was always that form.

When we have formed a thought, that thought seems real. It may even seem, if we are in a bad mood, that life is really not worth living—or that the kids are out to make life miserable, or that the spouse is being particularly difficult, or that life is unfair, and so on. While we can never experience anything but our own thinking, we can begin to understand the process by which Mind, Consciousness and Thought create the contents of our world. Once this understanding is in place, we can move more gracefully out of the world created from insecure personal thought.

The Principle of Consciousness

Consciousness is the ability to be aware of reality and of how reality is created. In operation, the three Principles cannot be separated; they are all part of an integral whole. Without the power of Consciousness, we would not experience reality. Without Thought, we could not survey life. Without Mind, there would be no life force or energy to bring our thinking to life. The more deeply we understand Consciousness, the closer we come to our souls, to pure understanding and the innate intelligence of Mind.

From early childhood we develop a self-image or self-concept—a set of ideas about who we are, what life is like for us; or what we have to accomplish to prove ourselves or to survive. Because of the way that the Principles *bring our thoughts to life,* we may start to think that these ideas about ourselves—about what we need, about what we can or can't do—really are the truth.

We start to accept these ideas about how we need to defend ourselves or live up to a self-image. We think that our ideas about how we can best cope with life are real. We then become immersed in that reality to an extent that this self-limiting set of ideas is all we see and all we experience.

Consciousness will make our particular thoughts our immediate reality. If we are hungry, we notice every restaurant on the street, even though we may have gone down that street before and not noticed any of them.

Elsie Spittle recalls: "When Roger and I were doing a training session at a local university in Tampa, we had agreed to meet at a nearby restaurant called Bennigan's for an early lunch to go over our agenda one last time prior to the training. I arrived at the restaurant on time and waited for about 15 minutes. When Roger didn't show up, I started to get irritated and think to myself, 'How inconsiderate of him to be late before such an important training session!' I waited a few more minutes, then called Roger's home. There was no answer, so I decided to order lunch. While I ate, I continued to worry. Perhaps he'd had an accident or car trouble, or perhaps he was just late. My stress continued to escalate. When the waitress brought my check I asked her if there was another Bennigan's in the area and explained that I was supposed to meet my friend there and he was quite late. She looked rather puzzled and said, 'But Madam, this restaurant is Chili's, not Bennigan's. That restaurant is a mile down the road!' Then I saw the name Chili's on the check she presented to me. The menus also had that name on it, and as I rushed out the door I clearly saw a huge sign reading Chili's. I hadn't seen any of this before. I thought I was at Bennigan's, so that's what I saw. It was

absolutely amazing to me that my thinking and consciousness had created a believable reality for me.
When I arrived at the 'real' Bennigan's, there was
Roger, who was worried about my being late and wondering if I had been in an accident. We had a good
chuckle and much more understanding about the power
of Thought and Consciousness creating personal experience of life."

The Principle of Thought

We human beings have been given a wonderful gift.
That gift is the power to think. Using this power, we
paint the picture of our lives. Like a talented artist, we
continuously construct the fabric of our outlooks on
life using Thought. Using this power, everyone has
learned to interpret and view their lives in their own
unique way.

Based on our unique life experiences, we all have our
story line and plot. But as soon as our thinking
changes, this plot, the nature of our story lines and
our realities, changes. Most of us don't realize how
this thought process works. Much of our thinking is
invisible to us *as* thinking. It looks more like a brick
house than a pile of bricks… it looks like reality. In
actual fact, this reality is like "smoke and mirrors," an
illusion created from a process we cannot see. Starting
to actually see the "behind the scenes" to the operation of these three Principles is the key to having a
personal choice in the quality of individual reality.

Thinking is something everyone does all the time. Most
often we are not awake to this fact. We are not aware of
the flow of our thinking in the same way that we are not
aware of our breathing. What we are aware of is our

resulting perceptions (how things look), our emotions (how we feel), and our behavior (what we do).

How things look, how we feel, and what we do are effects of Thought.

Imagine a person's thoughts as trees. If you are lost in the forest, the trees seem endless and you can't see any way out. If a helicopter lifts you up over the trees, you see the entire forest. You can see the "big picture" and the way out of the forest.

Educating people about the role of Thought is like lifting them up over the forest. Just as the forest still has trees, people still have their previous ideas and beliefs. No one can take these away from them, but they *can* gain a new perspective.

If you are watching a movie, for example, you might be totally engaged by the picture, briefly thinking it was real. At that moment, you would forget that a movie projector running the film is the source of what you are seeing. Most of us walk through life thinking that our "movies" are real.

Whatever we experience as "our lives" is determined by how we think. This is why two people can be in the same situation and perceive it differently. Someone can live in a subsidized housing development and be grateful for the opportunity to have low-cost shelter, to stop worrying about where he will live and get on with meeting the other needs in his life, such as education, job training and day care. Another person in the same situation might perceive that he is sinking downward, that he will never get out, or that he doesn't like the kinds of people he must live around. With this bleak outlook, he might lose motivation and hope and end up not doing anything with his life, sliding further downhill.

You could have two youngsters from the same impoverished family, brought up the same way but with very different outlooks about their opportunities for education. One is bound and determined to go to college, so he actively pursues and wins scholarships. The other sibling may feel he's "hard done by" and that life owes him a living. With this attitude, he will likely not be motivated to pursue his education. Again, it is his thinking about the situation that prevents him from seeing the same opportunities that his brother sees.

Thought is the ability to create images in our heads. The three Principles, working together, make these images appear real.

Mind, Consciousness and Thought are constant in this formula. As long as we are alive, we are always thinking about or aware of *something*. If we feel paranoid about what our neighbors are doing, the neighbors' behavior is what we notice. If we are grateful for what someone is doing to help us, that is what we notice. The variable here is *the content of thought*.

At the risk of saying the same thing to the point of being repetitive, the authors want to remind you again that the three Principles presented in this chapter can't be understood intellectually. This kind of understanding—or "wisdom"—comes as a natural process of realizing something totally new, seeing a deeper dimension of life that had not been visible to us at all before. The next chapter will describe what this wisdom is and how it comes to us via the three Principles. In fact, it comes to us very naturally through the workings of these Principles when we allow our minds to work in the way that it was designed by nature to work.

One of the paradoxes in life is that we all have difficulty finding something that we *already possess*. The next chapter will attempt to clarify what that thing is so that it becomes recognizable, or at least more easily notice-able, in our everyday lives. Rather than giving advice or offering techniques for attaining more wisdom, the chapter explains a process in which one merely gets out of the way and allows wisdom to emerge from within. Chapter Three will take another step and link the Principles to both the different qualities of our think-ing and to our feelings. This link provides practical clues about knowing when we are headed into wis-dom—and when we are headed in the other direction, away from relying on our inner wisdom and toward depending more on our past associations.

50

CHAPTER TWO

A Universal Intelligence:
Common Sense/Wisdom

*"Spiritual Wisdom lives within the consciousness
of all living creatures."*
—Sydney Banks, *The Missing Link*, p. 127

When we feel "up against it" in life, when we see only
barriers, frustration, unhappiness or despair, what is
it that has the power to help? The answer is not to
be found in merely changing our situations, even for
the better. Many people change jobs, location, partners and lifestyles many times over without ever
changing the quality of their thinking. If their outlook does not change, they will repeat the behavior
that caused the problems. They may change their
situation or location only to remain in the same state
of mind.

The answer is not to be found by going back and trying to figure out where we went wrong or what happened in the past. Genuine, lasting positive change
stems from tapping into an inner resource that allows
us to see a new answer, to access our good feelings
and wisdom in order to see the light at the end of the

tunnel. This chapter will describe this inner resource in terms of both its characteristics and how it comes to the surface.

Wisdom: The Equal Opportunity Employer

The good news about these discoveries is that we don't have to struggle or suffer to gain the wisdom needed to show us how to live a happy life. This wisdom is universal. It is as free as the air around us, and it is always trying to get into our brains, just as the air is always coming into our lungs so that oxygen can be distributed throughout our bodies.

> *Wisdom is constantly available for use by every human being on earth.*

Sages, philosophers, scientists, inventors and artists have tapped into this wisdom to inspire and create. Addicts have tapped into this wisdom to see the destructiveness of their habit and have stopped using, without long-term interventions. People have had changes of heart suddenly, after or during a disaster or life-threatening disease, that showed them how to live a happier, more rewarding life.

The human mind is designed in such a way that people are able to tap into and use this wisdom for their own benefit, *once they are aware of its existence.* In fact, this wisdom is always trying to resurface to help people live a saner, more productive life. The questions that first come to mind when hearing such a claim are, "If a universal wisdom is always available, why are so many people unhappy and suffering from emotional distress?" "Why is there so much conflict, miscommunication and resentment in relationships if we all have access to the same wisdom?" "Why is there racism, war and cruelty in the world?"

The real answer is that humanity hasn't delved far enough into how Mind works to turn our thinking into reality. Because Thought isn't widely recognized as the fabric of our personal worlds or as a logical product of the three Principles, we have only identified and learned to respect *certain kinds* of thinking. If the thinking we respect comes from the past, all we can do is recreate that same past. The key is to recognize and respect other innate capacities of the human mind and understand how they work.

Deeper Capacities of the Mind

In our natural, healthy state of mental functioning we have access to the entire range of the mind's capacities. Everyone has the potential for using their memory, their intellect and wisdom altogether in a compatible and constructive way. Insight and wisdom can surface at any time to enhance the use of memory and intellect. The authors have observed parents in families where there was child abuse begin to see easier and more effective ways of dealing with their children. Residents of crime-infested neighborhoods began showing the police how to reduce drug trafficking in their neighborhoods and teaching the schools how to improve the impact of discipline policies on their children's attitudes and motivation. Homeless, drug-addicted Vietnam veterans have realized that they have bought into the belief that they are unliked, worthless and rejected by society; the authors have seen these vets change their outlook and move into happier, more satisfying and responsible lives.

None of these people lost their memories or any of their intellectual capacity; they saw past experiences and the other things that had been familiar terrain from a new vantage point. They experienced insights that put all the information they already had together in a new way. One powerful example of this ability is a homeless man who had lived on the streets in San Francisco for more than 10 years. He was extremely hostile and aggressive, prone to threatening others with a machete if they crossed him in any way. As part of the county's homeless program, he began attending a weekly class on the three Principles. He became an advocate for the rights of the homeless, but was still angry and frustrated even though he participated in demonstrations and marches on city hall.

Once this man began to quiet his angry, resentful thinking, he began to see the viewpoint of the city and county officials and agency heads more clearly. He soon realized how to approach them to get a more positive response to his ideas. He knew how to get them to pay attention to how he and his homeless friends saw the needs of the homeless in that city. Within three months he had been asked to serve on the Mayor's Advisory Council on the Homeless and as a consultant to the Homeless Coalition. He was affecting policy and programs at levels ranging from grassroots agencies to city and county government. He was using his memories and *what he already knew* about the needs of the homeless in conjunction with wisdom in a productive way.

He later stated, at an interagency training session, that he could never have accomplished these goals if he hadn't been exposed to the three Principles, allowing him to realize how to tap into his own wisdom.

Accessing our wisdom and allowing it to be our guide can only help us to more effectively use our intellectual capacities (whatever they may be) and our memories in ways that benefit ourselves and others.

How Does Wisdom or Insight Surface?

There are quite a few fascinating published research studies from different kinds of therapy. These studies show a remarkable consistency, whatever the approach to therapy. Even in very different methods of counseling or treatment, change doesn't happen as a gradual upward process—it comes in bursts of understanding, in flashes of insight or as an instantaneous upward shift in people's feelings and thinking about their lives. Lasting change always seems to happen when a person is "struck" by a new thought. People generally describe these new thoughts as an "a-ha" realization. These insights provide a perspective that is more appropriate and helpful than the way they had been thinking about their lives before. While some people might attribute these shifts to something outside themselves, the authors contend that they are evidence of natural wisdom.

Our Sanity Comes and Goes

No matter how depressed someone has been, no matter how cynical or paranoid, no matter how disturbed and unhappy, they have moments—even days or weeks—of sanity, well-being and common-sense thinking. Because psychology has focused, understandably, on the treatment of dysfunction, these times have been viewed more as aberrations or flukes than as evidence of an underlying "saner" state of mind that is attempting to resurface.

In fact, multiple pilot projects have shown that most people slip into this healthy mode at times without even knowing it, such as when something distracts us from our problems or we are doing something we enjoy. We are having a good time, so we don't have problems on our minds. At this point, we often have a shift in perspective that makes our problems seem more manageable. Or we may see an easier, better approach to resolving problems that we hadn't noticed while we were gripped by old habits of thinking.

There is real power behind these moments or periods of health. One of the authors' clients shared this insight: "No one in the construction company I worked for liked the boss. He treated people badly and demanded too much. I suddenly realized that I knew enough about the business, and about how to treat people with respect, to foster the loyalty and motivation needed to start my own business." This insight led to a very different life for a construction worker who was once so insecure that he found it hard to keep a job. Now this man is a well-respected management consultant who travels all over the country helping corporations create healthy, productive workplaces.

These shifts in perspective don't take time. They happen out of the blue and *outside of time*. They happen because a very natural capacity of the mind is doing its job, the way it is designed to do it. This natural insight is one of a great many functions of which the human mind is capable. Our minds' "built-in" functions include the capacity for memory and for analysis, for processing data or information with the intellect. Yet they also include the capacity for insight and creativity, as well as for common sense. These are part of our natural adaptive/reflective ability to keep things in proper perspective. In this natural state, the proper use of Mind is automatic and all of the mind's capacities are accessible. This natural, healthy state is shown in Diagram One below.

Range of Capacities of the Mind

Wisdom
Insight
Common Sense
Perspective
Analysis
Processing
Memory

Diagram 1

Wisdom
Insight
Common Sense
Perspective
Analysis
Processing
Memory

Diagram 2

What Blocks Our Capacity for Wisdom?

If insight is a natural function, somewhat like breathing or a heartbeat, why doesn't it happen more often? Why do many people seem far removed from the ability to change their minds through having an insight? It appears that we lose sight of the most natural, beneficial, relationship between these various functions. We do this by learning to use our minds almost solely in a mode of thinking that relies on memory and processing our learned thinking, using the intellect without wisdom. In the state of mind in which we are immersed, or at the effect of our personal thinking, only analysis, processing and memory are available. We have blocked access to wisdom, insight and common sense, as illustrated in Diagram Two above.

When people are in a state of mind that relegates their thinking to processing known data from memory, they will have difficulty changing their outlook. If a person has been treated as unattractive in his past, he will continue to feel and act unattractive. If another person never felt good enough to please her parents, she may feel anxious or resentful around people in authority. If people grew up in an environment where others looked down on them, they may feel inferior. If they felt, as children, that they had to show off to get attention, they may continue to feel this way as adults. The perceptions and the accompanying feelings produced by these thoughts may grow to a point where mental illness or social deviance begin, not because people are products of their past but because they don't know that *it is only a habit of thinking that is keeping that reality alive.*

The Mind's Immune System:
Building on a Tendency for Health

Many people have insisted that the authors are being too simplistic in saying that chronic misery, anxieties and worries are merely habits of thought. They complain that they have tried to get these kinds of thoughts out of their head, but that the thoughts are too compelling and real to them. The authors' advice would be to stop trying to get them out of your heads. Even while these thoughts are still distressing you, you can gain perspective by *recognizing* that they are no more or less than ingrained ways of thinking picked up in the past. The wedge this perspective builds between us and these patterns of thought provide a gap or window through which our healthier thinking, better feelings and wisdom can sneak in like fog or smoke from a campfire coming through a window that is slightly ajar.

A helpful way of explaining the dynamics of this process is to use, as an analogy, the body's immune system and to look at how it fights off disease. The body has its own internal capacity for resistance and it naturally produces chemicals that fight off disease. If this capacity were not present, we would not get over the flu or any other illness. This capacity is innate and it effortlessly moves us back toward a state of health. We trust this capacity because we know that we are not defined by the flu, or by any other illness we may have at the moment. We are more than that, and we recognize that our natural default setting is health rather than illness. Therefore we trust that, if we rest and don't keep pushing ourselves, our more natural state of health will return.

In this state, our organs and functions work together in harmony, the way they were designed to work. The lungs provide oxygen to the blood, while the heart pumps it through the body, enabling other organs to do their work. Just like our bodies, our minds are always attempting to utilize each of their functions in a synergistic way that produces stronger mental health.

Strengthening the Mind's Immune System

Strengthening the physical immune system helps the body fight off a wide variety of diseases. In much the same way, strengthening the mind's immune system helps people ward off many different types of emotional problems. It also helps them use their own inner resources to see that they are capable of solving their own problems. The discovery of this innate ability to rebound with our natural mental resiliency provides hope for everyone. No matter how bad things look, if we can quiet our thinking we will regain access to the wisdom we need to make things better.

The most lasting way to help people strengthen their own psychological immune system is to help them understand how the mind can work to regain its balance. For example, if Bill is always fighting and arguing with his boss and has lost several jobs because of it, the authors would not try to directly address the behavior but would instead intervene at a more basic level, teaching Bill how the human mind works to produce the kinds of thoughts that justify his behavior and keep him in the emotional state that produces anger, hopelessness or fear. He could then learn to recognize the difference between this learned habit of thinking about people in authority and his healthier perspective, which emerges when these thoughts do not seem as real to him.

If Bill learned how to calm down and allow his healthy thought process to emerge, perhaps he could then see his boss as just another human being with his own moods, worries and concerns. Bill would then see that it doesn't make sense to take his boss's behavior so personally. By learning about the role of the Principles, Bill is armed with the ability to change his perspective. Bill is able to see the entire situation more clearly. Healthier, more responsive and productive behavior would be a much simpler, obvious choice from this higher vantage place of health, secure feelings and insight. What Bill was able to do, in this example, was to let go of his attachment to his personal thinking, and allow the Universal Intelligence (wisdom)—of which we are all capable—illuminate his situation.

The Simplicity of a Deeper Answer

It may help to clarify what is meant by the term "Universal Intelligence." Science has traditionally considered intelligence to be something that originates in the brain. The Mind is much more than the brain. This Intelligence exists inside and outside of ourselves, in nature itself, in everything and everyone. Although this Universal Intelligence may appear elusive, most people sense there is some "power" behind life although it may seem difficult to recognize because it exists before form.

For example, a natural ecosystem functions with intelligence behind it. Without thinking or trying, trees tap into the energy of the sun and soil. Each species exists in a natural balance with other species. They instinctively know where to live, what to eat, how to reproduce and where to go to spawn. There is an elegant interdependence and homeostasis between the plant and animal life in a natural ecosystem such that it will always move toward balance and harmony. None of the plants or animals has to figure out how to do all of this. They do not learn, in school or from their culture, any beliefs or intellectual ideas about how to relate to one another or any other species.

Human beings have access to a similar natural intelligence. It is such a ubiquitous, natural intelligence that we do not have to think about it or figure it out. Some people might call it wisdom, or the soul, or innate mental health. They all mean the same thing. They are words that describe the human connection to Universal Mind—a link to the source of wisdom, understanding, compassion and forgiveness. Mind is the divine gift that inspires and motivates us to continually reach inward to access our spiritual natures. We start the journey of discovery about our true selves by discovering the power of Mind.

The human mind is designed to work in harmony with this Intelligence. We can always function in a state of mind accessing a clearer, more tranquil mode of thought that allows us to receive and use this Intelligence. In fact we are always immersed in this Intelligence, whether we realize it or not. This Intelligence functions through the principle of Thought. A wiser thought could be about anything. It could be an employee seeing that his boss isn't an ogre, but that his boss is insecure and trying hard not to be labeled as incompetent. It could be an executive realizing that he has become such a workaholic that he isn't enjoying life anymore. It could be a parent realizing that her anxiety about a child doing well in school has created a harsh parenting style that causes the child to dislike school.

Whatever the specific realization, it has the quality of coming out of nowhere. People often report that these kinds of insights come when least expected. Leading scientists or inventors have stated that such moments often come when they become frustrated and almost completely give up on a problem—they stop trying to figure it out, take their mind off the problem, and the answer pops into their head. Former gang members report that they suddenly realize what they have been doing to themselves and walk away from that self-destructive life. Each of these people has connected to a healthier vantage point, one that gives them more wisdom and understanding.

While some of us can say that we have had this kind of experience, it seems rare to many and is certainly unpredictable. Most of us know how to consciously engage our intellects and try to analyze or solve a problem. Yet we do not know enough about how this inner Intelligence works to be able to use it all the time. Through the authors' experiences and work with thousands of people from all walks of life, they have observed that this Intelligence is always available. Everyone has direct access to this state of mind that brings insight, serenity and a constructive outlook for everyday living.

The next chapter will clarify the role that feelings and emotions play in day to day life. Feelings and emotions are presented as an understandable product of how the Principles work to create reality. Because feelings and emotions are a product of a Thought process, we can use them to trace our reactions to anything back to the *quality* of our thinking. Thus our emotional responses are an unerring gauge of the quality of our thinking at any time. They can be used to help us get back on the right path and to find increasingly deeper levels of wisdom.

Chapter Three

The Role of Feelings and Emotions

*"Our feelings are the barometer of our thoughts.
When the mind is filled with positive thoughts,
cause and effect rule, resulting in a positive feeling."*
(Sydney Banks, *The Missing Link*, p. 111)

How do we know how to differentiate between when
we use our thinking against ourselves and when we use
it wisely? How do we use this understanding in a practical way to begin to live *naturally* from the vantage
point of our inner intelligence? How do we know when
are we using common sense?

A healthier state of mind is first recognized by feelings
of ease, self-assurance, self-worth and contentment. It
is noticeable as a quieter, calmer state of mind. People
often call this feeling "peace of mind." It can come at
any time, but usually comes when we have nothing
dominating our thoughts.

These deeper, positive feelings are comparable to the
feelings we have when we are relaxing, enjoying a
favorite hobby or spending an evening at home with

the family. It is the opposite of the feeling of insecurity. We can know, *at any moment*, what state of mind we are in by noticing the quality of our feelings and emotions.

The Practical Value of Feelings and Emotions

There is a very clear, logical relationship between our emotional feelings and our thinking. Remember that each person's reality is created from the three Principles and built from Thought. Emotions and feelings are also produced by Thought. If a person has thoughts along the lines of, "I am no good... no one cares about me... life is hard and overwhelming," they will produce emotions in line with these thoughts. The emotion would be one of depression, hopelessness or frustration. *Feelings and emotions are a reflection of the way we experience our thoughts.*

Our Emotional Early Warning System

The real practical value of emotions and feelings is to tell us—in a *direct, accurate* way—how our thinking is working. The more negative our emotions, the more we are getting *warning signals* that we are caught up in our contaminated, insecure thoughts. If you are in a building and the fire alarm goes off, you leave. The alarm has detected signs of a fire. When we begin to feel hostile, anxious, or take things personally, these feelings warn us that the quality of our thinking is declining. Our wisdom tells us that we should retreat from the illusionary world we are creating with those thoughts. An emotion is always the result of a thought. The quality of the emotion equals the quality of the thought.

Thoughts Produce Feelings

Using emotional feedback about the quality of our thinking is tricky because our thoughts are trying to convince us that they are real, not misleading. If Sheila gets upset at her boss, she will be thinking that her boss is doing something that she *should* be angry about. If Bob feels lonely and frightened because he thinks his friends don't really like him, he may decide that he needs to move away or get new friends. It may not occur to Sheila or Bob that they are using old *habits of thinking* to distort the meaning of the fact that someone did not return a call right away or was too busy to go to the movies.

Understanding what our emotions are telling us gives us an understanding of the role of Thought in life. Recognizing how the quality of our thinking is *tied directly* to our feelings and emotions is *using that understanding* in the moment. Using this understanding is a powerful agent for change. It may take some courage and honesty, but as soon as we realize what is going on, the quality of our thinking begins to improve.

When people live with the belief that their feelings come before their thoughts, they are being fooled by the illusion of life. They think that their emotions come first, so they find reasons to believe they should legitimately be upset. They are giving their power away to circumstances, to their past and to others. In truth, a thought comes first, *then* we have a feeling. Without understanding, we may blame that feeling on someone or something we can't control. For example, an friend of the authors was recently attending a writers' retreat at a lodge in Arizona with two other writers from different parts of the country. One of these writers was a young novelist from Boston; the other was a nature writer from Minnesota. The authors' friend remembers:

> "While I was away for the night, the two other writers had dinner together. The younger writer was

eager to get to know the nature writer and probed the older man about his experiences in the wilderness. The young novelist also asked if he could read something the nature writer had written. The older writer, who is something of a loner, had suffered through a long day answering e-mails and urgent phone calls. He firmly stated that he wasn't in the mood to talk and they ended the meal in silence. Two nights later my daughter came to dinner with all of us at the retreat. The nature writer and she had an animated, intense discussion about investigative journalism and their experiences covering environmental stories. When my daughter left, she asked the nature writer if she could borrow a copy of *Outdoor* magazine that she had spotted.

"By that time the younger writer was furious, taking the nature writer's seeming dismissal on the earlier evening very personally. The younger writer concluded that the older author did not like him. In this frame of mind, he also assumed that the magazine my daughter took was given to her by the nature writer because he had written a story in it that he wanted her to read. After my daughter left, the young writer came into the living room very upset, saying he was going to go home a week early. At that moment, he couldn't see that the nature writer was often in a mood in which he did not want to socialize and was sometimes in a mood in which he did. His reactions had not been personal in any way. The magazine had neither belonged to him nor contained a story by him.

"The young writer, without knowing it, had created all these negative feelings in his imagination. If he had never realized that they came from his thinking, he might have left and not been able to finish his important writing project. Fortunately, I was able to share some funny examples of these kinds of misunderstandings from my own life, coming from a feeling of compassion for both of these exceptional people and their different interpersonal 'habits.' During the discussion, the tone lightened up to the point where this young author had an insight that provided him immediate relief from his hurt feelings and a good laugh for all of us. Although I was somewhat in the middle of this situation, I was able to keep my bearings by staying neutral, seeing each of them as innocent, feeling loving toward them and maintaining a sense of humor."

This man was able to help the younger writer because he maintained his impersonal, deeper feelings. He wasn't tempted to take sides or make himself unhappy with thoughts along the lines of, "Why are they getting into this garbage when I am here trying to relax and enjoy this retreat?" or "They are ruining this for me" and so on. Because he avoided judging anyone or reacting personally, he was able to use his wisdom to diplomatically show his colleagues a way out of a potentially destructive situation.

When people hear stories like this one, they often ask why it feels so hard for them to stay in that less personal stance. It is because their self-image or ideas of what is important to them are being threatened. These images or standards are themselves made up, and they only interfere with the natural use of wisdom. Chapter Ten will explore the way this misuse of our thinking has an impact on the quality of relationships. Even though we may feel that we have legitimate, compelling reasons for being upset, all we are really doing is generating "static" that interferes with our wisdom and keeps the problem around longer.

Understanding Deeper Feelings

Living in the experience of deeper feelings is how the mind is designed to work. When we live in our natural, healthy state of mind, we experience feelings of well-being, peace, happiness, contentment and enthusiasm. We experience whatever we are doing as fascinating and challenging. An insight or realization, an "a-ha" moment that produces an answer to a vexing problem, invariably comes with a positive feeling. At the very least, insights provide a feeling of relief. Insights lead to creative ideas and to improved relationships. Such insight can be simple: Perhaps the marketing director suddenly sees a whole new way to promote his company's product. A businessman may discover a simpler way of organizing his work, allowing him more time to better supervise his staff. A wife may realize that her husband is irritable because he had a hard day at work, not because he doesn't love her anymore.

Even in situations in which someone has said something hurtful, or appears to have done harm to us, we will have more understanding and not take things personally if we see that situation from a healthy vantage point. If we view that person or situation from our personal thinking, we have no choice but to see only what they have done to us, and to feel hurt, angry or upset. All we have access to in this state is our insecure thoughts and we often can't help taking it personally.

If we are in contact with our wisdom, we can see the situation from a more empathetic viewpoint. We might realize the other person was feeling threatened or reacting to events from within the framework of his insecure thinking. We may realize that he was seeing the situation differently and acted based on what made sense to him. He was not intentionally trying to do harm.

From a healthier vantage point, we are less tempted to take things personally. It is more obvious that people always behave in a way that makes sense to them. They're doing what they think they need to do to survive or manage life. The vast majority of the time, people's behavior has nothing to do with us. They are simply doing what seems normal or appropriate to them *in their world*. Understanding the role of Thought makes this apparent. People react with behavior that stems from how the situation looks to them. They behave in ways consistent with their thinking. Recognizing this allows us to feel compassion and understanding rather than taking their behavior personally.

If we are able to stay in our wiser mode of thinking, we see a way to respond that will help a person calm down. We might see a way to help someone engage her own common sense. Staying on her side, we may find a solution that will benefit both of us. Rather than getting angry and frustrated, we can see that she is living in a reality that causes volatile behavior to appear compelling or necessary to her. If a two-year-old child puts her hand on a hot stove, or sticks her toast in the VCR, it doesn't help to get angry. We know that she does not know any better. Everyone is innocent in this same way. People do what they do because they feel it is *their best or only choice,* given how they are thinking.

Understanding Psychological Innocence

One of the most profound shifts brought about by an understanding of the Principles is an enhanced ability to recognize "psychological innocence." Another way of describing this shift is to say that we can more clearly see how a person's behavior is the only thing that made sense to them at the time they behaved the way they did. This is not to say that people don't behave every day in ways that do harm to themselves or others. No one can deny that violence in the world harms innocent people. No one can deny that parents sometimes abuse their children, that police sometimes bully citizens, that people commit crimes or that bosses have been known to mistreat members of the workforce or behave in a harsh way that destroys an employee's self-respect and motivation.

Nevertheless, the authors truly believe that people always make what appears to be their best choice, given how they interpret their situation, the possibilities or options that seem available, and how they evaluate their own abilities *at that moment*. We may know that there are some people who make what we consider to be bad choices from a moral or practical standpoint. Yet if we were living within their world, we would see their behavior quite differently. We might see that they felt under attack by a hostile, uncaring world, that they were feeling depressed and resentful about a perceived injustice someone did to them, or that they were feeling desperate and felt that they were fighting to survive against all odds.

Whatever way that person is viewing his or her situation looks real to that person. The more upset or "gripped" they are by these thoughts, the more real those thoughts appear. Seeing this fact about everyone stems from understanding the principles of Mind, Consciousness and Thought. The logic behind these Principles demonstrates that everyone's thoughts look real to them, whether they are what we would judge to be rational or irrational.

When people are in more insecure, less objective states of mind, they are acting out of desperation or the feeling that they are in the right and everyone else is misunderstanding or misusing them. In a healthier state of mind, these thoughts, feelings and the harmful behavior that stems from them would not make any sense.

The conclusion to be drawn from this discovery isn't that we should let people off the hook or fail to hold them accountable for their actions. The real implication is that when we understand the Principles, we can more easily lift ourselves and other people out of that overwhelmingly negative view of reality. We can't help anyone see their situation from a less desperate perspective if we judge or criticize them.

Forgiveness and Change

When people see their own psychological innocence, they forgive themselves. In doing so, they are not trying to get off the hook, but rather they are allowing themselves to move out of the world of guilt and resentment—and the recurrent behavior that keeps this cycle alive. They are released from feelings of shame, regret and self-doubt. Once crippling thoughts and feelings are gone, people feel better. In better spirits, they can look more objectively at what made sense when they did the things that led to those feelings. But now they can think more clearly. What happens, as a result, is that those same behaviors don't make sense anymore. When people's unconditional self-respect comes back, their common sense and wisdom increase automatically along with it. They can leave the past behind and walk into a healthier life.

Deeper, more beautiful feelings are the route to wisdom. It is nice to know that we are not being self-indulgent or irresponsible when we enjoy ourselves. The more we allow ourselves to get fully into the things we like—to the point where we forget about ourselves altogether—the more we open up our minds to moving into a higher level of consciousness. At every new level of consciousness, we have more wisdom and less insecurity. Thus, we are less likely to do harm to another.

During a Principle-based project in Southern California, the authors were working with a program for the homeless. One of the clients was an African-American Vietnam Vet. He had fought in Southeast Asia and returned to find the war unpopular at home. He started to believe that, rather than a returning hero, he was an evil person who had done something bad. He started to feel guilty and ashamed, turning to alcohol and drugs to drown these feelings. Soon he was either too depressed or too high to work and found himself homeless. He managed to survive on the street for almost 20 years. Finally, he dropped into the homeless shelter and attended a program based on the Principles. During this initial exposure, he realized that all of his depression, guilt and low self-worth stemmed from the way he had interpreted his experience of returning from the war in Vietnam. He said that as soon as he realized that it was his own thoughts that were creating the lingering problem, the thoughts shifted and he felt better, more carefree and relaxed than he had ever felt before. He found a new outlook on life.

He decided to stick with the program. He soon moved into temporary housing, quit drinking and using drugs, and got a job. He was later hired as an outreach worker and trainer in Principle-based projects by the same organization that had helped him get off the street. He has now helped a great many people out of the situation he was himself in only a year before. His story has inspired others who can now see the possibility of changing chronic, long-term habits of behavior and getting on with their lives.

When shame, regret or resentment seemed unavoidable, this person could not get out of the cycle of drugs, homelessness and depression. When people live with these desperate feelings, they often try to bury them. Have you ever noticed, for example, that when you attack or confront someone about their behavior, they normally get more defensive or justify it more rigorously? In their eyes, you are not pointing them toward more responsible behavior but are attacking their fragile world. When people sense that their well-being comes from within, they can cut through all their posturing and their memories to go right to their common sense.

Forgiveness is a central theme in spiritual teachings from all religions. Genuine forgiveness, based on seeing the fact of psychological innocence, clears the decks both spiritually and psychologically. This perspective gives people a second chance without making them feel like perpetrators or like victims. When people feel that they are being allowed a fresh start and are treated with respect for their innate wisdom, that wisdom is much more likely to come to the surface.

One common question asked about the idea of not judging people's behavior is, "How will society control people who are out of control? Won't people do whatever they feel like doing?" The answer is that we do need to control people who are a danger to themselves or to others. We need jails and mental hospitals and other settings that protect people in society from harm. We also have to realize that we are, at the same time, protecting people in these settings from themselves.

However, prisons and psychiatric institutions would be different places if the people placed there were treated with deep respect and a real knowledge of their potential. Simply stated, *people change when they feel better*. A fundamental change in a person's outlook is always a prerequisite to changing their behavior. People can change their outlook more easily when they feel secure and safe, when they don't feel they are "up against it." When they are not feeling under attack, they can consider new possibilities. Otherwise, they are themselves in the worst prison of all—the prison of their own hellish thoughts.

The common wisdom is that people are most likely to change when they hit rock bottom. Because everyone's innate health or inner resources are buoyant, most people will resurface whenever they stop defending or trusting their current thinking. If they hit rock bottom, they may open themselves up to their deeper feelings and wisdom. It is like someone who is drowning and struggles in the water until he gets tired and stops struggling. He may then relax in the water and find that he can float quite naturally.

When we give up the stubborn attachment to our learned habits of thinking, we can make things easier for ourselves and others. We can do this by realizing that there is something just a thought away from what we already know—an insight that can empower us to change our entire outlook. Wisdom is the capacity that allows people to live up to society's highest values without having to struggle for caring, positive and responsible behavior. Such people merely see cause and effect differently than they did before.

Without self-judgment, it is easier for people to recognize that they actually live within the quality of feelings they are expressing. They are also better able to see the big picture of the long-term personal consequences of their actions—as well as what they are doing to others—from a more compassionate, less desperate vantage point.

Forgiving Ourselves First

Seeing our own innocence also helps us recognize the same innocence in others. What we must see is that at those times in the past when we have done harm or hurt others, our behavior made sense to us at the time. Our motives were not about wanting to hurt someone else for the sake of doing harm. At the time, we probably felt that some injustice or harm had been done to us that justified what we were doing.

How We Block Our Deeper Feelings

Many people say they would love to have more peace of mind, to be more calm. Most would love to enjoy life deeply, living productively with contentment. It is satisfying to have a life of contentment and self-respect. And in actuality, these feelings are always just a thought away. They return automatically when we drop the thought that they are not appropriate or possible at that moment, or that they are not available in a particular situation.

Many believe these feelings are both rare and dependent upon specific circumstances. People say they have these feelings on vacation or when their children are being helpful and cooperative, when they get a raise and are told they are doing a great job, and so on. Others say they have these feelings when they are jogging, reading a favorite book or playing cards with their closest friends.

What keeps us separated from more peaceful feelings is the thought that we cannot feel peace in this or that situation. The block is our *thinking about the situation,* not the situation itself. An instructor for a Principle-based project recently asked her students when they felt most relaxed and at ease. One person said that it was when she was at home with family, just hanging out. The next person said he felt that way most at work, doing a job he enjoyed. He said he felt ill at ease and anxious at home because he worried about being a good provider, father and husband. The third person said she felt happy and relaxed on vacation, while the next person said he got restless and anxious on vacation, but felt better back at work where he felt he was useful and productive. Someone else said she only felt relaxed and contented when she was reading a mystery novel because she could get lost in the story and stop thinking about her own life.

Because our deeper feelings are innate and resilient, they are always trying to get back to the surface. When we can quiet our thinking and are open to accepting a beautiful feeling, the feeling will come. These feelings are not tied to anything except our thinking. Unfortunately, most of us are not told this as we grow up. We are told the opposite. We are told that we must have something (money, a nice car, clothes or an attractive partner), or do something (win a game, be the smartest, toughest or funniest person in the room), or become something (a college graduate, the best lawyer in town, the leader of the gang, most popular in the class) to feel good and worthwhile.

Our feelings are an indicator of our state of mind. Whether we think in healthy or unhealthy ways, our emotions will be tied directly to what we think about. Parents may feel that they failed a child because they did not play baseball or other sports with him when he was younger. With this thought come feelings of inadequacy or guilt. The parents may think about a time when the child asked for help with a problem in high school and they were able to help. They might then feel gratified or appreciated. At that moment, they feel better. One of the parents may then have a thought about not finishing a project at work on time and suddenly feel frightened about being called on the carpet by the boss.

When we use our thinking in this way, we ride an emotional roller coaster. When we realize the deeper feelings that are natural to us in our wisdom, we can get off the roller coaster. We can feel calm, relaxed, clear and alert in any situation when we know how to access our healthy thinking. Once we recognize our wisdom and understand its value, we seek to regain it even in the midst of upsetting, stressful or potentially harmful situations.

A parent in a Principle-based program for high-risk families had a terrible temper. She screamed and yelled at her children whenever they did not mind her and she felt they deserved it. She was angry and upset almost constantly. She came to the parenting classes primarily because her daughter's behavior was getting worse and she didn't know what else to do.

The parenting classes discussed how everyone gets upset or angry at times. The group talked about how these feelings are accompanied by criticism, blaming and judgmental thoughts. These are often the times we feel like lashing out at our children. The instructors discussed how when we stay calm, we are able to see how to help our children learn to use their common sense.

This volatile woman learned to calm down, to see that she had a tendency to lose it and go off on her children. One day she got a call from school informing her that her daughter had been caught stealing. She immediately became furious, running to the school to scream at her daughter. On the way there, she remembered what she had heard about calming down and taking a new view. She picked up her daughter and didn't say a word to her all the way home. She told her daughter to go to her room. Then the woman went to a neighbor's house to calm herself down. It took her two hours to stop feeling angry and distraught.

When she finally did calm down, the woman began to suspect that her daughter had her own fears and anger. She went home with a different attitude and truly listened to her daughter, trying to be helpful by showing the girl how to use her common sense in the situation. The outcome astonished her! The daughter quickly came around, felt much better, and found new solutions to her problem. The mother later reported what she learned: When she was upset, her common sense "went right out the window!"

Once the parent began listening and stopped reacting to her child, the daughter felt more comfortable sharing her life with her mother. The two became fast friends. That young woman is now in college and doing very well in her studies.

Stepping Back to Regain Perspective

Natural intelligence can provide a new frame of reference from which to evaluate any situation. It enables us to step back from the immediate problem and get a clearer view of the best way out. When we understand how Thought creates feelings and emotions, we can disengage more easily from personal thoughts and memories that cause us pain and learn how to wait for a better feeling to return. When that feeling comes, it will come with insights that illuminate the best course of action. The way out will be more obvious through higher quality thinking.

The following chapter will look more closely at the nature of insecurity and at the kind of learned thinking that keeps us separated from our natural wisdom and healthy outlook. If we know what wisdom is—and how accessing our deeper, Universal Intelligence feels—it becomes easier to notice when we are caught up in insecure, deeply ingrained habits of thought. The next chapter should help the reader to see more easily how insecure habits of thought are picked up throughout life by everyone, and how to see through this smoke-screen to access wisdom via Universal Intelligence.

CHAPTER FOUR

Insecurity: The Illusionary Barrier to Wisdom

You have probably realized by now that the most important thing is to tap into your own natural intelligence. This intelligence offers a useful, healthy perspective that helps you view life with clarity and positive feelings. This vantage point is inclusive, in the sense that once you discover it, you easily find all the desirable emotional qualities you need to enjoy life and to live within a world of appreciation, fascination and engagement. It is your innate intelligence that enables you to live life with these feelings while you naturally use all of the attributes of your thinking, from intuition, wisdom and insight to your intellectual and analytical learning.

Few would argue that self-respect is not a good thing. Few would argue that positive motivation helps, that empathy for others and compassion are worthy qualities, that self-assurance, enthusiasm and the ability to listen are admirable traits. These are qualities we would love to pass along to our children.

The key is to let these feelings get stronger in us as a result of using our natural intelligence. Then we cannot help but pass them along to others.

Universal Intelligence provides the perspective for youth growing up in a hostile environment to see that they can succeed in spite of circumstances. It helps a teenager see that he or she would get along better with the parents by being interested and helpful rather than sullen and resistive. It helps teachers see, through realizing that every student wants to learn, how to get more out of students by engaging their curiosity.

This intelligence shows business leaders how to get the most out of people without burning them out. It shows couples how to forgive and come to peace with each other's foibles and habits. It gives people direct access to the deeper beauty in life. If all these wonderful qualities are available to all of us, why do so many of us have such a hard time in life? Why do we approach life so seriously? Why do we let things that are not important get us so upset?

The Source of Insecurity

This chapter describes how insecurity can limit potential. Insecurity is not a necessary by-product of life circumstances but *originates in our thoughts*. Understanding the source of insecurity, that it is a habit of thought, increases our ability to realize our potential for a healthier life. Seeing how insecurity works helps us realize exactly how it blocks our potential for intelligent functioning. Then we can recognize our insecure states of mind and move out of these limiting states to regain perspective. This chapter will address the question of how we know when we are experiencing life via insecurity and how to find the way out of a maze of insecure thought.

Insecurity hides in the form of *learned thought*. One of the most important steps in helping people to regain their healthy perspective is helping them understand how learned thought determines their outlook. Many people have strong habits of thinking that are self-defeating or even self-destructive. These thoughts look real to them and contaminate their outlook on life every day. They feel defeated and frustrated most of the time.

As with the body's immune system, these contaminants lead to a state of unbalance. People can become too depressed to look for work, too nervous to study, too upset to think clearly. Realizing that insecurity is merely a habit of thinking loosens insecurity's grip on us and helps us gently let go of our contaminated thinking. Our balance then returns.

The authors' clients—whether they are executives, housewives, residents of low-income housing, adolescents, parents, teachers or anyone else—almost invariably begin to realize that they *can* regain their balance. This realization enables them see a glimmer of hope during times of adversity. Only then can they evaluate their situation with common sense and see the most helpful thing to do.

It is important to help people realize that the vantage point of common sense is not related to any learned point of view, opinion or belief that they might have picked up from their past, in the home or during their schooling. Many of these ideas, beliefs and expectations are the things that keep us insecure.

For example, if a child is always put down at home, told he is stupid and treated as a bad person, he likely takes these beliefs to school. As a result, he might cut up in class to avoid studying. He might feel anxiety that interferes with his grasp of a subject. He might fall behind and feel even more stupid. As a result he might feel alienated and not see the point of trying to do better.

If the same child realized that his behavior came from insecure habits of thinking, habits that were self-defeating, he could see the possibility for doing better. He might become more hopeful. He could start to relax, pay more attention and apply himself. He might then turn his situation around.

We must understand that this realization does not come from a person's past. It comes from an *insight*—something new, something unrelated to how an individual thought in the past. It comes from seeing a connection between past-related thoughts and present behavior.

What Makes Up Our Personal Viewpoint?

Using the Principles and free will, all of us create our personal perceptions and interpretations of reality. If a person's perceptions cause bad feelings of fear, inadequacy or hostility, he is putting insecurity into action.

For example, one parent might see his child as a burden and a bane to his existence. Another might see his child as a source of delight. These two parents are likely to treat their children in totally different ways and may produce children who see life very differently. The first parent may have children who always feel that they are a burden to others or a need to prove they are worthwhile. The children of the second parent are more likely to thrive on life and live with less self-consciousness.

The good news is that people don't have to go back and change what their parents did or lament how they were treated. Once people understand that insecurity is thought—and that thought changes moment to moment—they have the freedom to start each day, each moment with a clean slate. It is only when people don't understand this that they innocently use their thinking against themselves and other people in their world.

Leaving the Past in the Past

Many current models of helping or counseling take people into their past to explore where problems started. The assumption of these models is that we are damaged goods if negative things have happened to us in the past. The most logical thing to do, according to this model, would be to try to go back and somehow repair that damage.

Therapy, counseling and educational applications based on the Principles have shown that thinking about the past in a certain way—not the past itself—is the real problem. Neither our wisdom, nor our potential for well-being and common sense, are damaged by the past. These resources are untouched by insecure or self-conscious thinking patterns.

Each person's past exists only in the confines of their memories. It is not even the memory of trauma or negative things in the past, but what we *made* of them that caused the damage. Our bad feelings now are a result of how we interpreted them, or what we *decided* these events meant about us and about our futures.

If we dwell on thinking about how we were abused as children, how a teacher told us we'd never amount to anything, or how our parents said that we weren't any good, our current states of mind are affected. These thoughts become our outlook, our self-image, *now*. We are likely to see our children in the same way and pass the same perceptions on. As we start to understand how our thoughts contaminate our experiences, we begin to drop the attachment to ingrained habits of thinking.

When we use our innate common sense, we gain the wisdom to avoid dwelling on abuses that happened in the past. In our healthy thinking, these thoughts don't harm us because they come and go and don't permanently impair or contaminate our current outlook. They do not bury our common sense. Insecure, negative thoughts from the past only harm us when we allow them to create static or interference, like a radio signal blocked by static coming between us and our natural wisdom.

Are There "Thoughtless" People?

We wonder about people who seem to have no remorse, even after killing someone. Others might be stealing, dealing drugs to children or harming themselves and others in different ways. Some would call these people callous, thoughtless human beings. This is not the case; the problem is *the way* these seemingly remorseless people are thinking. Such people have learned to think in a manner that is so utterly negative and hopeless that they cannot tolerate their own thoughts. They are liable to live in a numb, unfeeling reality, void of real satisfaction or hope.

Their reality is not at all thoughtless, but produced by thinking from their conditioning or alienated frame of mind. They unwittingly use their own thinking to create a hell for themselves and then fight that hell everyday with their behavior. These people endure thoughts that tell them that life is stacked against them, that everyone is working to make life harder for them, that they have to struggle every day to prove they should even exist. They often numb these thoughts with anger or resentment and a drive for immediate gratification.

This is not to say that the way anyone thinks is better or worse than how anyone else thinks. If we look at thinking neutrally, we see that the ability to think about our lives is like any other power. When it is used with understanding, it is used productively. We use it to learn, to become wiser, and to master more aspects of life.

Using Thought Against Ourselves

This same power can be misused. It can be used to make us feel despondent, bitter, fatalistic and even homicidal. Even when we can justify or defend thoughts of blame, anger or revenge, we are still using our power to think against ourselves. We are the ones living in these feelings and seeing life as unfair, hopeless or overwhelming. We can blame and justify forever and never escape these feelings and their consequences for us. The trick is to know what our feelings are telling us, and to have the courage and wisdom to drop our negative thoughts so that we can approach life with more understanding and more hope.

Here is a story that illustrates this fact. One of the residents from a public housing community with which a project team was working had led a very tough life. Thelma's three adult children were in prison and she was appointed as primary caregiver for her two grandchildren. She took good care of her grandchildren and, when they weren't in school, she brought them with her wherever she went. Elsie recalls the first time she met this woman:

"She was intimidating—very angry, with an 'in your face' attitude. I wasn't sure what to make of her, but I was pleased that she was coming to our leadership program. She was considered a key leader in the community, so I knew that if Thelma heard something that would improve the quality of life for her, the whole community would benefit.

"She often brought her grandchildren to the leadership meetings. If they misbehaved, she immediately got very angry with them and would threaten to beat them—and she would sometimes give them a swat upside the head.

"I wasn't sure how to handle this. She didn't really hurt the kids, but the behavior and the example she was setting were hardly conducive to learning. Thelma continued to come to the meetings and gradually began to change. Her face softened and she became gentler with the grandchildren, not as quick to react. She became more active in their schooling—meeting with their teachers, helping them with their homework—and soon you could see the children changing, becoming better behaved and better students.

"At this point, we were about to start a youth leadership program at the request of the resident council. I wanted to hire one or two residents to work with our staff so that ultimately we would leave the residents in charge of the program.

The idea popped into my head, 'What about Thelma?' So we hired her, letting her know that she would require more in-depth training to learn how to share an understanding of the Principles with the youth.

"Thelma didn't express much feeling for the opportunity she had been given, and I was curious about that. I thought she would be pleased, but she was very matter of fact, as if this opportunity was no big deal.

"The youth program started and seemed to be going well. In addition to Principle-based activities, we had the Sierra Club provide field trips. Staff, parents and children had great fun. It was amazing to see the children thrive on the love and attention given them.

"However, I began to hear stories about Thelma and how she was reverting to her old habits of threatening to beat the kids, only this time she was threatening children in the youth group. I didn't know what to do and was experiencing a variety of negative emotions—disappointment, indignation and judgment among them. I decided that it was time to talk with her, so I called and invited Thelma to lunch.

"Knowing how important my own health is and that rapport would be crucial to having a heart-to-heart talk with Thelma, I felt even more stress. By the time we met for lunch, I was very anxious. She was a big woman and very intimidating. Once our food order was taken, I hemmed and hawed for a few moments, then went for the direct approach. I told her I,wanted to talk about the youth program and that she might not like what I was about to say, but that it was important we talk. I really wanted to hear how she saw the program. I also told her that I had been very nervous about meeting with her.

"She looked startled at my admission, and then we both relaxed and began to talk. It was a wonderful, heartfelt conversation. I began to see that she had no idea how intimidating she was nor did she realize that her habit of threatening the children was inappropriate. To her, it was commonplace and natural; she didn't mean anything by it and would never dream of following through. The threats were just her way of getting the kids' attention. As we talked through lunch, we came to a 'meeting of the minds' and felt closer to one another. Before she left, she hugged me, which was surprising because she was not a demonstrative person. She had tears in her eyes as she told me no one had ever said she was intimidating and that it had opened her eyes to her behavior.

"After we parted I reflected on our meeting and realized that Thelma was full of positive feelings, but that she just didn't know to express them. She wasn't thoughtless or devoid of feeling; she just didn't realize the value of thoughts and feelings or perhaps didn't trust them because she had been so deeply hurt in the past.

"Thelma continued with our youth program and never threatened the children again. Then she went on to become a teacher's assistant at the neighborhood school and also a parent trainer.

"That was a powerful example for me to trust my own feelings more and to gain a fresh appreciation for their value. Using my feelings as a guide accessed my common sense and courage so that I was able to talk with Thelma, despite my earlier insecurity, and handle the discussion with integrity and diplomacy."

While it may seem difficult—or even unreasonable— to stay in a caring, neutral stance in some situations, merely knowing that this state of mind is the one that you want to move toward, and trusting the natural buoyancy of that state, will help greatly. The following chapter will explore in more detail how discerning the operation of the three Principles helps make these results happen more often, more predictably and more naturally.

CHAPTER FIVE

The Benefits of Teaching People About the Three Principles

Just as an experienced house builder can teach a young apprentice how to build a house from blocks of concrete, people can be taught the operating Principles that define how all of us as human beings *build our individual realities from Thought*. People then know how to use this beautiful gift—their birthright, the gift of Thought—in a positive way. They know how to change their mind. They know how to change their world in the direction they want. As well, they know how to distinguish between their biases, beliefs and expectations from the past and their common sense. They know about and appreciate their natural resiliency. They find the ability to maintain their stability and well-being in any situation.

When people do not understand how these Principles work in relation to their own thinking, they are at the mercy of the ebb and flow of their thinking. In low moods, for example, they may see their children or spouse as the enemy, as monsters who are making them miserable. This thinking can lead to family violence or abuse. Based on earlier experiences in life, they may be afraid to return to school, or feel that no one wants them in their company, or that they can't trust anyone, or that they need to worry about everything that might go wrong.

When people tap into their common sense, they feel more giving, loving and secure. The next day they could get caught up in insecure, unhappy thoughts and consider giving up. Without any understanding of the role of these Principles in creating reality from Thought, people can't grasp why they have shifting moods, why they go in and out of different emotions and ways of seeing their lives. Their thinking, emotions and behavior seem out of their control.

When people recognize how the Principles function, they find that they always have a choice about whether or not to see things through the filters or contamination of the ways they have learned to interpret things from their past experiences. They know they can choose to see with common sense, with new eyes, with a fresh, insightful and more responsive perspective.

Our Natural Wisdom

This capacity for wisdom is with us all when we begin life. It is a natural perspective that allows us to use the entire range of the mind's capacities, as shown in Diagrams One and Two (in Chapter Two). The vast majority of children function in this way naturally, until they start to take on the contamination of the thinking of people around them. Children are naturally motivated. They are innately curious about life. They are into mastering their world and learning how things work. They learn and change rapidly.

In a national survey of young children, 95% of eight-year-olds said that they could dance, sing, write poetry and build things. Interviewed 20 years later, only a small percentage said they could do any of these things. As we grow up, we accumulate conditioned thinking that tends to become self-limiting.

Although humans appear to lose touch with their childhood enthusiasm, we can't ever lose access to this wisdom. Each time someone has an insight they are in touch with their wisdom. There is a freshness, a vitality to wisdom that allows us to keep an open mind and learn new things. Because young children are naturally in this state much of the time, their learning curve is rapid and they are constantly becoming new people who are more mature and more capable. Wisdom is the source of common sense, objectivity and good judgment. It is the only way we can see things new, or have an "a-ha" moment when we see a situation with deeper understanding.

Our Intellectual Functions

Although this book is focused on wisdom and insight, you should not infer that the intellect isn't useful or important. Processing information and analyzing data from the intellect *is* useful. This built-in capacity is natural as well. It is designed for a specific purpose. It is where we store and retrieve information, processing it to do things so that we do not have to learn them all over again. For example, once we learn to ride a bike, we don't have to relearn it every time we get on a bike. The same thing is true for driving a car, getting to work and home again, doing math and so on. Used in the way it is supposed to be used, the processing capacity is helpful and necessary in life. Used in the wrong way—against ourselves—it can be our worst enemy!

When this processing function is doing the job it is designed to do, it can be very helpful. You may have heard people say things like, "On the way to work, I was thinking so much about this new idea for the project that I didn't even think about my driving or where I was going, but suddenly realized I was there—I had somehow arrived at the office." This example shows the intellect, memory and insight— all available to us in our wisdom—working together, as they are meant to do. We can then free up our minds to take in, think about and have insights about other things.

With an understanding of the Principles behind reality, people will recognize how they get themselves in trouble in life when they start to rely on the processing function most of the time. Because this aspect of our thinking does not include insight or original, creative thought, we are limited to what is stored in memory. We keep processing the same data and the same thoughts over and over. We become stuck in a limited, circular and eventually stale way of functioning. Without an understanding of the function of Thought, we are not aware that this trap of circular reasoning is our thinking in action. We may conclude that life is hard; we may attempt to keep coping and responding in the ways to which we have become accustomed, ways that come from our familiar habits of thought rather than from our common sense or natural intelligence.

Learned Thinking

Learned thinking is memory, processing or "personal" thought. We are extremely fortunate to have a memory. Memory contains a great deal of useful information, not the least of which is language. It would be inconceivable to have to wake up each morning and relearn the alphabet and the rules of grammar.

Memory helps us in the process of analysis. Let's say it was your job to choose which accounting system your agency should purchase or you were figuring out your income tax. These tasks require utilizing learned information about math stored in your own computer—your brain. Although a good deal of information stored in memory is useful, all of us have a significant amount of distorted, untrue, questionable, negative data stored as well. Trouble arises when we rely on this data to tell us how to look at and feel about life.

Insecure Habits of Thinking

Babies are not born with negative thoughts about their lives. While some babies may seem "fussier" than others, no one is born into the world thinking that their self-worth depends on his or her skin color or station in life. No one is born thinking that they have to be athletic or brainy or well dressed or popular with the opposite sex, or any other "conditional" idea about what they need to be happy. As soon as babies are born, however, they are exposed to the beliefs, ideas, opinions and perceptions of the people around them. They pick up ideas and expectations from the people, the community and the society in which they are raised. These ideas become implanted or programmed into their memories.

Psychology usually refers to this kind of learning as conditioning. All this means is that we learn to think in set ways about life, from the outside in. Up to now the field has recognized and tried to work *almost solely* with the content of thought. Because psychology, as a field, has not realized that ordinary people can utilize these Principles to understand how their thinking works, and because everyone has been conditioned to think in certain ways, the best that mental health professionals have been able to do up to now is try to recondition or reprogram people's negative, insecure, conditioned, "outside-in" thinking. Such professionals are innocently caught in the same trap, working from outside in, starting from behavior rather than from the Principles.

For example, if parents in a family are angry and tend to respond to situations with violence, their children learn this habit. If parents worry about things, children learn habits of worrying. Because children think this is normal, they accept violence or worry as a natural part of life. Negative conditioning is like a contaminant or a pollutant in our thinking. If we fill a clean fishbowl with muddy, dirty water, the fish inside will see the whole world as made up of dirty water.

Conditioning to the Extreme

Many of the youth with whom Principle-based projects have worked in inner city communities or in public housing already had contaminants in their thinking by the time they entered the first grade. Many thought they couldn't learn that teachers were against them, that they wouldn't be popular, that they would have to fight to have any self-respect. These thoughts might have been picked up at home, in the community, from the media or other sources. These thoughts made them feel like they were just marking time in school, so why should they learn if they could not possibly be successful?

There have been many real reasons for these youth to feel this way. Many were born into a race or culture that has long been subjected to discrimination. Many had a rough childhood in homes with a lot of fighting and instability. Many had already suffered disillusionment and rejection. If they had continued to think in this way about their lives, some could have ended up in jail or wounded—perhaps even killed—in a gang war.

Nevertheless, a person's mental health is determined at each moment by how *they hold their experiences* in their thinking. In these early intervention programs, the young people learned that their moment-to-moment outlook is always a result of the quality of their thinking. They learned that they had a real choice—to hang on to their current attitudes and alienated outlook, or to make these thoughts less important.

Seeing Health and Innocence
The staff in Principle-based programs respected the psychological innocence of the youth and showed compassion and respect for what they had gone through. They realized that the young people were doing what made sense to them, doing the best they could do to function while saddled with thoughts that looked real and compelling to them. This stance helped the youths calm down and see that they were not bad people and that someone understood their world. They learned about the Principles, which were being taught in youth leadership classes or as regular classes in the schools. Grasping the logic of these Principles was just like learning addition. Recognizing this logic led to an understanding of how their reality was formed, which in turn released their inborn capacity for using common sense and thinking for themselves rather than being led by peer pressure. Merely knowing they had this capacity gave them hope that they could change their lives. They were taught about natural self-esteem versus a learned self-concept. They started to see that if they went through life trying to continually prove themselves or live up

to any self-concept, such as being tough or "too cool to care," they would be stuck in that dead end world forever.

To their own surprise, the young people started to feel good and enjoy themselves without having to posture or act a certain way around others. Curiosity and natural interest in learning came back gradually, and they started to do better in school. They were becoming more responsive and respectful even though they were hardly aware they had changed. Many of these young people are now in college; others are building careers around their chosen vocations. When asked about their past lives in gangs, dealing and using drugs, they would merely say, "I am not that person any more." It wasn't a big deal to them—this change was so subtle and natural.

One young man who had been a gang leader in South Central Los Angeles had this to say: "I don't really know what I learned about my thinking. I started to change because Eddie Mae (the Project Coordinator for the Community Empowerment Project in his neighborhood) believed in me. She saw the good in me. When she saw me walking in the community one day, she stopped me and invited me to a resident meeting. She respected and accepted me, even though I was wearing my gang's colors. When I attended the meeting, most of the other people accepted me, too. They asked for my ideas about a community event they were planning. At first I didn't trust them, but after we worked together for a while and they used my ideas, I liked hanging out with them. My 'homeys' wanted to know what I was doing at these meetings, so they came to check it out. Now I'm a role model for good in the community, rather than for bad."

When Principle-based projects began in public housing programs in Florida, the project staff took the time to listen and to develop rapport with the residents. The staff found that many of the residents were constantly overwhelmed by their daily lives. Their self-esteem was low. They felt that they already had three strikes against them. Many thought that because they were minorities, because they were poor, because they had dropped out of school and were on public assistance, that there was something wrong with them and that they would never do any better.

Buying into these thoughts lowered their mood levels and introduced depression, hostility and fear into their daily routines. These thoughts and feelings colored their views of their neighbors, their children, their social worker, the police and housing management. Most had given up hope for a better life. As they regained access to their common sense or wisdom, they started to see their past as just that, the past. They began to learn from it and to have new insights about how to move their lives, their families and their community toward a more positive direction. One of the women became a powerful, effective leader and was appointed to the mayor-led Miami Coalition. She stated that an understanding of the Principles "didn't give me anything I didn't have, except to let me know, and to bring out, what I already had inside of me."

The Relevance of Memory

Natural intelligence or common sense does not deny the past, or the fact that people have had traumatic experiences or gone through very hard times. Common sense shows us when to use memory in a productive way and when it simply does not help. We should use information we have already learned when that data, stored in memory, is relevant. In other words, when using common sense, we turn to memory when it is needed and helpful. We don't dwell on or bring up memories if they take us into a painful state of mind. We can learn from the past, or keep *repeating the past*, depending on the perspective from which we view it. We always want the ability to look at things fresh, with the notion of insight or discovery. If we can access this common sense, we begin to function in a more mentally healthy way.

Most people rely on memory far too much. They dwell on resentments, jealousies, fears and hurts about things that have happened long ago. They carry a self-concept from the past in a way that keeps them closed to new experiences. They worry about the future because they can't see beyond thoughts about their past. All of these thoughts burden them, lowering their spirits so that they have a hard time enjoying life and living *now* by using common sense.

You may have heard people make statements such as, "that's water under the bridge" or "there's no use crying over spilled milk." These common-sense sayings may sound trite or hard to live up to sometimes, but they are true. When we start to see what healthy functioning is, and begin to experience that state of mind more often, these ideas seem obvious and leaving the past in the past seems much easier to do. When we are not living in a state of psychological health, these same things can seem much more difficult, not at all obvious or simple. The key is to understand what healthy functioning is and what it involves. The following chapter explores healthy functioning more fully and relates it to how each of us experiences our everyday lives.

CHAPTER SIX

Living in the Zone: Everyone's Birthright— Healthy Functioning

Our Birthright: Wisdom and Well-being

The Principles provide the only framework in the field of psychology or any of the helping fields that defines mental health with a depth of meaning beyond eliminating our symptoms. This paradigm has identified health as more than controlling symptoms, as more than simply the absence of distress or even the ability to successfully "cope" with stress. In itself, innate mental health is the antidote that heals these symptoms. It is also the capacity that enables people to live and work in what has come to be called "the zone."

The three Principles, as they function together, show us that mental health is living naturally in a state of well-being with the absence of chronic stress or distress. This state of mind is everyone's birthright and is always potentially available, no matter where we are or what we are doing. Knowing this allows us to move back into compassion, gratitude and understanding—even in situations in which others would think such behavior impossible.

Many people think that certain circumstances make it impossible to stay in a positive state of mind. The authors have known people in prison, people who were on bridges in earthquakes and in other desperate situations, who kept their bearings and common sense. Because they were able to do this, they could use their wisdom to enhance their chances for survival. People are able to maintain their calm and well-being, *irrespective of their situation*, if they know how the Principles work.

Functioning in the Zone

After Tiger Woods blew away the competition to win the 2000 British Open, everyone was speculating about how he could manage so consistently to stay in what athletes call "the zone." Woods had just done the same thing at the U.S. Open, which had been played at Pebble Beach, one of the most difficult golf courses in the United States. This ability to stay relaxed and focused to fully use his natural talents was so remarkable that it prompted cover articles in both *Time* and *Newsweek*. The *Newsweek* article interviewed well-known sports psychologists and researchers who had studied "the zone" as a state of mind. They had a variety of theories and techniques that they used to help people get to the zone. The three Principles show us that we are already, naturally, in the zone as soon as we quiet our insecure thoughts.

The important thing to realize is that it is *always* insecure thinking that takes people out of mental clarity and secure, adaptive distancing from their situation. Athletes will somehow slip into the zone and suddenly play more effortlessly—far beyond their normal game—yet with the same pressure and competitive situations going on around them. Most athletes would love to know how to attain this zone more of the time. The trick is in knowing that our minds always wants to go there because the zone is our natural default setting. What we need to learn is how our unrecognized, insecure thinking takes us away from that naturally healthy mental state.

In Principle-based programs with police officers, the initial phase of the training was designed to help the officers see that people in the community could be treated with more respect. Officers began to see that by doing so they could gain more cooperation from citizens. These ideas were introduced into the curriculum as part of the officers' course work on community policing.

The officers found that understanding their *own* thinking—and how to bypass their conditioned habits of reacting—allowed them to stay in a clearer, more responsive mental state. Then they could see, beyond appearances and their own biases, how the situation looked to the other person and why that reality seemed important or compelling to them.

The police were particularly grateful to experience this alert, responsive state when they were in dangerous, life-threatening situations. They found themselves able to stay calm but with a heightened awareness of all the elements of any situation. They responded in ways that defused these situations. They were able to be firm, command respect and calm things down, rather than reacting in ways that added fuel to the fire.

People often report that in a crisis or disaster situation they find themselves suddenly calm, automatically knowing what to do to help. A woman who is a friend of the authors was on a bridge during an earthquake and actually saw the bridge collapse in front of her. She started to get frightened—and then realized she was okay and that others needed her help. She got out of her car and started to calm people down and assist them in getting off the bridge before the rest of the structure could collapse. She stated later that she was so grateful to be in a calm, compassionate state that she was not afraid or even anxious about her own safety.

Being in the Zone

Many of us have experienced being in the zone while working out at the gym, playing tennis, walking on the beach or holding a newborn baby. In this state, the right moves seem obvious and simple; we feel in harmony with the world around us, part of a bigger whole. In this state it does not matter what the obstacles are or who our opponents are. Dr. Mills reflects that, "There have been many times that I have played someone in tennis or racquetball who is a better player than I. If I get insecure thoughts in my head about that fact, or worry about being skunked, I immediately get out of my rhythm. My shots won't go where I want them to go, and I feel awkward and out of synch. As soon as I forget about who I am playing or drop the need to prove skills or ability, I am back in the flow of the game and shots and movements come back naturally. The irony is that once I begin to care less about winning than I do about simply enjoying the game, I have sometimes gone into the zone and beaten better players."

One of the most exciting things
we can realize as human beings is that
the mind is designed to function in a healthy way.
We interfere with that process with insecure thinking.

Most athletes would love to be able to play their sport in the zone all the time. Yet how and when they access this state seems mysterious to them. Dr. Mills played college football with an athlete who performed in the zone 90% of the time. His name was Roger Staubauch, a quarterback who was an All-American in college and went on to have an NFL Hall of Fame career with the Dallas Cowboys. Dr. Mills remembers: "As I got to know Roger, I realized that, in addition to being an incredible athlete, he was able to keep things in perspective. He never took himself or his fame seriously. To him, football was always a game he enjoyed—and he approached it in that way from high school through his professional career. In his mind, the last two minutes of the Super Bowl were no different from scrimmaging with his friends in a pickup game. The pressure and crowd noise were not part of his world."

Knowing How It Works

A mechanic who has memorized the repair manual and follows it by rote to repair a customer's car is never as good as the mechanic who genuinely understands how the engine works and how each engine part plays its role in relation to the entire process. A good mechanic relaxes her analytic thinking and gets into her "zone." She then has a direct feel for the entire motion and dynamic of the engine's operating principles, and can often tune into the source of the problem just by listening to the engine run for a few minutes. Such mechanics seldom need to rely on a repair manual.

Knowing how reality stems from the Principles is all that is needed for people to move back to where they began their lives, to this state of graceful, wise, insightful, productive thought. Happiness and common sense are our birthright. We give away this birthright when we start to think about something in a way that the world might say is "normal." It isn't normal, for example, to have good feelings if we are in jail, or in prison and so on. However, we have to produce a "memorized" thought about the situation to feel any other way. A memorized thought is one that we learned from our cultures, families or society as a whole.

Letting Go Into the Flow of Life

We have all heard stories about people who have transcended their circumstances to help others or do things people think of as extraordinary. Artists and other creative people report a mental state where ideas just come to them. Musicians love the feeling of jamming, of getting tuned into each other's wavelength during a set and going beyond where their music has taken them before. They describe the feeling as being "in the flow of music," tuned in naturally to each other's rhythms. Most people have experienced times when they felt in harmony with life and were moving with the flow of life.

Elsie recalls the time she first made a presentation to a group of professionals: "I was nervous because I'd never spoken publicly before. Wondering what on earth I could talk about, I took my place on the stage. As I looked out at the audience, all of a sudden I felt calm and words poured out of my mouth. The audience was very attentive. I lost track of time and before I knew it, people were applauding and my presentation was finished. That was an incredible experience of being in harmony with life and seeing that when insecure thinking is quiet, natural wisdom emerges."

How the Mind is Designed to Work

What has not been recognized until now is that being tuned into the flow of life is the way the mind is designed to function. The "naturalness" of this state is what causes it to come back when we expect it least. This naturalness is what sometimes prevents this state from coming back when we try to elicit it via a technique, such as meditation or guided imagery, or with a familiar ritual like jogging, gardening or yoga.

Because of the power behind Thought (described in Chapter One), one way to keep our inner wisdom at bay is to think that we lost it and that we need to find a way to get it back. It is impossible to lose. Yet any thought that gives us the feeling of insecurity will take us away from that state. Insecure feelings draw us back into our personal worlds and create static or interference that obscures connections to this more natural, healthy state of functioning.

Understanding the Principles keeps us on course because we now know the origin of our minute-to-minute experience of life. We know that our experiences come from *inside our heads*. When we combine this understanding with a recognition of how the Principles operate together, we will start to live in healthy functioning.

In healthy functioning:

- We will be aware that the quality of our feelings and emotions reflects the quality of our thinking
- We will navigate moods without doing unnecessary damage to ourselves or to others
- We will not take on chronic stress or negativity
- We will be able to escape feelings of helplessness or distress by moving back to our wisdom
- Using our wisdom, we will eventually come up with solutions for life's dilemmas, answers that provide positive outcomes.

As helping professionals, the authors personally know hundreds of citizens of disadvantaged neighborhoods—from Miami and Tampa to the South Bronx, from Minneapolis to Oakland, San Francisco, San Jose and South Central Los Angeles—who live in this natural state. These people found the fruits of their resiliency while they were living in crime-ridden, drug-infested communities. In every community where the authors have worked, as soon as a critical mass of people began living in a natural state of health, they began using wisdom and personal power to change their communities.

Each of these neighborhoods is now a community on the move toward substantially less crime, less drug abuse, fewer teen pregnancies, fewer school failures, less child abuse, less family violence and less unemployment (Health Realization Institute, April, 2000, "Summary of Clinical, Prevention and Community Empowerment Applications"). These communities are changing from the inside out, not from external interventions. They have become truly empowered.

The Ordinary Quality of Our Natural Intelligence

For some people, ideas about "inner wisdom" or being in the zone seem ephemeral and impractical. A more down to earth, practical way to grasp the reality of this intelligence is to see that it is merely common sense. There are people we think of as having a lot of common sense. What this observation normally means is that they are usually able to look at situations in their lives with good judgment; they don't get carried away on flights of fancy, nor do they emotionally overreact to adversity or take things too personally. They tend to listen well and to be helpful to others when friends are irrational or upset. They see practical, realistic ways to move their lives forward.

The authors' experiences with a wide variety of communities, cultures and types of people have clearly shown that everyone has an inborn capacity for common sense. This type of intelligence is what makes resiliency possible. It is an intelligence that is different from the kind we measure with IQ tests or grades. This natural intelligence comes from the same source in everyone, and everyone has it.

When we see this natural intelligence in action, it looks like maturity, sound judgment or "savvy." It does not come automatically with experience or age, but it can be used to learn from our experiences. Once people know they have common sense they also have hope. They know that no matter how bad things look to them, there is hope.

Common sense provides perspective, objectivity and mental clarity. This kind of intelligence is also the source of insights and of creative, original thought. Call it a practical, "gut level" wisdom that helps us understand how we work and how our lives work. This understanding brings with it a solid state of well-being, feelings of unconditional self-esteem, and the motivation to get on with our lives.

This intelligence is the basis of natural mental resiliency. It is this intelligence that is always trying to resurface to help us solve our problems. This intelligence is not something we obtain through pre-set methods or getting advice from others. While we can read or hear stories about the results of people using this intelligence, we cannot get the intelligence itself from any story or from a description of how someone else triumphed because they used their wisdom.

The Route to Wisdom: Quieting the Mind

Engaging our common sense or deeper wisdom is not a learned process. It does not result from analysis or thinking about our problems. Rather, this kind of thinking occurs to us or bubbles up in us without effort. It bubbles up when we clear our heads and have less on our minds. A study was recently conducted, asking hundreds of CEOs of large and small companies when and where they had their best ideas. The top three answers were: in the shower, in the car and on vacation. When a person's mind is relaxed, when he or she is not dwelling on a problem or straining for a solution, insights come.

One client asked the authors, "How long do I need to stay in the shower to have an insight?" We *cannot* force an insight. We can't make insights or common sense happen on command, like we can dredge up memories and analyze things. "A-ha" moments or new ideas and insights often seem to come out of the blue. They are most likely to come when we have nothing in particular on our minds. While it is impossible to have *no* thoughts in our heads, we can always move back into a calmer state where our minds are not as busy, and where thoughts "flow" rather than become "circular."

Maybe you've played a rigorous game of basketball or a challenging game of chess or have been working in the garden and noticed how quiet your mind was, noticed the gentler, more positive feelings that accompanied this quiet mind.

Chances are, at this moment, having absorbed some of what you've read here, your situation looks better to you, your goals attainable, your future more hopeful. Whatever thinking or planning that comes to you in this state of mind is likely to enhance your situation. We are all tempted to find answers by keeping problems on our minds and going over them time and again. Most of us have a feeling that this does not work, even though we do it. If we have faith in our innate potential for common sense, it is easier to let things go and know an answer will come to us from deep within our souls.

How to Live in a Quiet Mind

Once people quiet their turbulent analytic thinking, they find common sense, clear thinking and insight. They do not lose their ability to analyze or figure things out. They just use that ability more efficiently and appropriately. They not only resolve problems better, but also come to peace with them. They don't chronically worry or fret about things, but spend most of their time feeling contented and enjoying life. They are self-motivated from feeling challenged and interested rather than being motivated by fear or a need to prove their worth.

If these benefits of living in a quieter state of mind are so rich, why aren't more people drawn to this state? First of all, most people aren't familiar with and don't trust the idea of having a quiet mind. They feel they have to stay on top of everything by going over and over their various problems and their situation. They don't trust that their wisdom or common sense will alert them about when to pay attention and when to relax and get their mind off of details.

Secondly, most people don't know that the mind will naturally move toward this state or that the state of meditation is the most natural condition of the mind.

People think they have to meditate or get themselves into an altered state through an activity or focusing of awareness (e.g., repeating a mantra, breathing exercises, martial arts). All we have to do is point in the direction of our innate health and common sense. We must also realize that worrying about how we are doing is not productive. Worry only exacerbates the problem. When we regain a quiet mind, we find that this state doesn't entail having a mind empty of all thoughts. Because personal reality *is* thought, we are still having thoughts. What we are having is much *higher quality* thoughts. In a quiet state of mind, insights, wisdom and contentment are the characteristics and qualities of thought that come to us. This is where the solutions to our problems come from.

The capacity for understanding life better:

- Is always potentially available
- Can be used without reliving or struggling with the past
- Is in everyone, regardless of their circumstances or history of problems.

The next chapter will explore the implications of recently published, long-term studies and show how this research points to an inner source of resiliency. The chapter will describe how our resiliency comes by way of an understanding of the three Principles, and will also describe how the illusionary barriers of insecurity inhibit the ability to experience resiliency and create positive changes in our own lives, in relationships, in work and in communities. This research also points us right back to the buoyancy of our innate mental health as discussed in this chapter.

CHAPTER SEVEN

Innate Mental Health: The Source of Resiliency

The Buoyancy of Mental Health

The authors' experience has shown that each person's innate mental health, in the form of well-being and self-sufficiency, returns automatically. It is always trying to establish a foothold, just as the body is always marshaling its resources to fight off disease. It regains a foothold most quickly when people know *how reality is formed, moment to moment, via the three Principles.*

The idea of resiliency has gained a great deal of attention in the prevention field. This attention is based on results of longitudinal studies done over 20- to 30-year periods. The research reveals that a large percentage of youth, all of whom grew up in highly stressful, dysfunctional families or environments, were able to rise above their conditions. The majority grew up as healthy, responsible adults, regardless of cultural and ethnic backgrounds. These studies have led to new interest in the notion that people have a natural tendency to rebound and regain their equilibrium, which in turn has resulted in the popularity of health promotion approaches.

Resiliency is the capacity that allows people to become free from the grip of their circumstances. It empowers people to choose their own outlook and not be as adversely affected by things outside themselves. The basis for resiliency is that our natural good feelings, mental health, always want to come back, much like a cork bobs to the surface. When these natural good feelings return, our wisdom and common sense return with them. All these attributes come from inside, from our deepest psyche. These capacities supply the resiliency needed to change our circumstances for the better.

While more and more people in the helping and human relations fields are impressed with the research on resiliency, they still rely on the traditional paradigms to design their interventions. Thus, the approaches they design are based on putting resiliency *into* people from the outside in. The missing link to our inside-out source of natural, innate resiliency is understanding the Principles. It is knowing that every reality is created from inside out. Recognizing the connection between Thought and behavior enables us to see where behavior originates, in Thought. This recognition helps us see through the erroneous assumption that behavior is a product of anything other than our thinking about that situation.

Resiliency and Our Everyday Thinking

Our circumstances and how we view or respond to them are two different things. We can react blindly from anger, fear, depression or self-pity. Or we can be more reflective and insightful, using common sense to see ways to improve matters, make the best of things, or change the circumstances if possible. The human mind can operate in both of these ways.

If a person's mind is functioning in a way that produces negative thoughts, it makes sense that this person will also experience negative feelings and self-destructive behavior. The opposite is also true. If someone's mind is generating positive, creative thoughts, that person will experience more positive feelings and positive behavior. Everyone's mind can do both.

The mind has a natural or built-in tendency to function in the more positive mode.

It always helps us to remember that a negative outlook is incorporated into our thinking from outside, in the same way that germs come into the body from outside. These intruders then contaminate the body's immune system. The body's immune system works from inside out to eliminate these contaminants. The mind's immune system does the same thing, administering wisdom and insight from within to help us eliminate the negative, self-destructive thinking that originally entered from outside. *This capacity is the true source of resiliency.*

It is important to point out that many people are currently living in terrible circumstances. Violence, poverty and prejudice take a toll on a growing number of men, women and children. No one would suggest that, if people look at these facts differently, their problems will disappear. It is quite possible, however, that human beings can overcome even the most horrendous situations once their natural tendency for health is rekindled.

The authors are certainly not condoning policies, cultural biases or prejudices that leave some of our citizens living in poverty, or living with chronic feelings of inferiority, paranoia or anger. In fact, the authors strongly believe that, if the people in the world as a whole reconnected with their innate mental health, with their wisdom and natural well-being, all of these adverse circumstances or unfair practices would quickly disappear. Using their wisdom, people would see how these injustices contribute to despair and more problems for us all. From within this same wisdom, people would see past their prejudices to a point where they could find ways to resolve these conditions.

The authors have found, in 15 years of community-based projects, that residents in the most deprived communities became the most powerful change agents. By realizing their own innate health, the residents became wise and resilient enough to take charge as visionary leaders. They established new relationships and worked in collaboration with societal institutions. Residents became empowered to establish new working partnerships with law enforcement, local government, social agencies, the media and educational institutions. Their confidence and thoughtfulness substantially altered how these groups viewed them and their potential. They were able to affect more enlightened policy and bring new resources and opportunities into their communities on a much larger scale than anyone thought possible.

The Route to Living in Wisdom
People don't have to worry about "getting" wisdom or practicing rituals and techniques to get wiser. This source of resiliency will always bounce back and resurface on its own. All you need to know is how Thought works to either unleash or block wisdom. Chapter Four explained that only a psychological

attachment to our learned habits of thinking blocks wisdom. Why do we all learn—and come to believe in—insecure thoughts that keep us in a cycle of negative or self-limiting thinking? Why do self-doubting or self-conscious thoughts keep us confused, upset, stressed or resentful much of the time? Why is it that this kind of thinking appears real and meaningful? When we get trapped in a negative pattern of thought, the feelings and behavior that stem from these thoughts lead to predictable, often familiar results. Yet we are so immersed in the reality produced by these thoughts at the time that we cannot see the forest for the trees.

Building Our World from Thought

One reason this more limited, self-conscious thinking grips people is that we all build up a self-image from the fabric of our thinking. This self-image then starts to look real and fixed just as when we build a brick house it starts to look like more than a pile of bricks. Once the bricks of a house are cemented into place, it takes on the appearance of a home. People do the same thing with their thinking.

People build an inner world, a reality that looks very real to them, even though it is made up of thought. This world looks so convincing that they take up residence in this "reality," even though it might be filled with pain, or lack of hope, bitterness and anger. While this world is built from personal thought, in the same way that the house was built from bricks, most people cannot see this. Once people discover the role of Thought, it frees them from this world of suffering.

For example, when Dr. Mills was growing up, nothing he did was good enough for his "perfectionist" father. If he set a school record for tackles in a football game, his father would point out the ones he had missed. If he scored 95% on a test, his father would be upset about the questions he missed. In college, even in graduate school, he always expected his teachers, coaches or mentors to disapprove and to focus on his failings. He would get so nervous while working on papers that he could not get his mental faculties organized. On most assignments he would waste time spinning his wheels to avoid work. In his early career, he experienced stress and second-guessed himself at every decision.

Dr. Mills realized that all of this distress and unproductive behavior was a result of a *habit of thought*. His father had never wanted his son to see himself as a failure. His father was doing what made sense to him, trying to give his son the discipline and whatever else he sincerely thought would help him be stronger in managing the "struggles" of life. As soon as the son saw *through the illusion* of the world created from that habit of thought, he began to enjoy and thrive on his work, becoming more efficient and productive.

A student at a Principle-based clinic in Florida was in treatment for drug abuse and depression. He had done well in high school and was the class valedictorian. Yet he started getting high every day and flunked out of the state college as a freshman. He became severely depressed and almost catatonic. His family was made up of high-level professionals who had advanced degrees from Ivy League schools. There were high norms and expectations for academic and career achievements. When he arrived at college and saw all the other bright high school valedictorians, he began to worry whether he was as smart as the other students and wondered if he could handle the course content. He began using marijuana to ease the effects of his fearful thoughts, started cutting classes, and spiraled downhill from there.

Both of these examples show the effects of insecure thinking in blocking the use of common sense. When these thoughts are seen for what they are—just habits of thinking that tend to build on themselves—they are no longer a factor. This young man came to counseling sessions once a week for three months, and learned how self-conscious, insecure thinking had caused his downward spiral. He also began to recognize the difference between real self-esteem and the insecure self-concept he had picked up from his family.

Within six months the young man was back in school, doing well and not feeling the need to compare or judge how he was doing. His common sense surfaced and he became more comfortable with who he was. Then he became interested in his studies rather than afraid of them.

Recognizing the Freedom of Thought

The factor that helped free people from these negative patterns was recognizing the three Principles at work. Once people see that everyone's world is completely created by these Principles, they find a simpler, more direct way out of pain or chronic suffering. No one's mind is limited to producing negative thoughts. Every human being has the capacity to think beautiful, inspiring thoughts or to think depressing or fearful thoughts. When we know this, we can experience choice over which quality of thinking we want in our lives, which we want to trust and value. The more we trust our wisdom, the more our outlook evolves in a positive direction. *Resiliency emerges with the realization that we can change our minds.*

The key to resiliency—to regaining our good feelings, self-respect and a positive outlook—is *not* to delve into the past to see where insecure thoughts and feelings started. The key is to regain access to our healthier thinking. We want to reopen our connection to insight and common sense, allowing us to recognize our thinking from the past as just a memory. Common sense shows us how to take our minds off ourselves, to stop thinking in a self-conscious, insecure way. We have the wisdom not to dwell or to blame the current situation on the past. In fact, we see the current situation completely differently from the perspective provided by common sense and insight.

The Ordinary Quality of Healthy Thinking

Up to now, access to this kind of wisdom, and to creative capacity and insight, has seemed to be available only to a few. In fact, authors who write about or point to this mental state talk of great musicians or inventors or exceptional athletes playing head and shoulders above their peers. Yet the authors' work with troubled communities, with middle-class citizens and with corporate executives has shown that this wisdom is ordinary and freely available to everyone in a much simpler, more direct way than any of us had ever realized.

Matter of fact wisdom is at work when a parent, for example, realizes he has been putting too much pressure on his child about school work, causing their child to dislike it, avoid it and even lie about having done it. With this insight the parent's perspective shifts. They then may be able to show more patience and help their child see that schoolwork can be interesting and fun, or challenging in a more positive way. Matter of fact wisdom may involve a person seeing that their alcoholic parent wasn't trying to make them unhappy or make them feel undeserving growing up. Rather they recognize that the parent was unhappy and struggling and was trying to cope with their own thoughts of fear, insecurity or shame. Thus, one simple insight can free that person from a lifetime of resentment, doubt or guilt.

What Wisdom Does

Psychology and the helping professions have historically attempted to help people by teaching them how to analyze their past. The field has developed and refined techniques to manipulate or reprogram behavior that is a product of the past. Wisdom is a much better solvent, leading to the most lasting cure for stress and distress. Wisdom takes us directly to the present. It clears our lenses, eliminating perceptions from learned habits of thinking. If the past comes up at all, in a state of wisdom we see it for what it is. We can see that it is only how we were inclined, or taught, to interpret and make meaning out of whatever events occurred to us in an earlier time. It shows us that we are not just the product of our past experiences, but have developed a certain "self-delusional" view of life as a result.

The philosopher René Descartes said, "I think, therefore I am." We are what we think we are. Whether we think we are a failure or a hard worker, whether we are shy or aggressive, if it seems like a given, that is the direction our lives will take. Our learned ways of thinking about ourselves—from childhood upbringing, cultures and so on—is only one view of what we are. Yet it is one that we continue to make up again and again, using the same power of Thought. With wisdom, we see this fact and recognize that we can make that personal perspective on things have as much, or as little importance, as we want.

> *Once our personal views of life*
> *can be distinguished from wisdom,*
> *they are naturally replaced by wisdom.*

Leaving the Past and Its Symptoms Behind

Prior to these discoveries about this inner source of resiliency, the entire field of psychology held the view that people are a product of their past and that we only had the resulting behavior and feelings with which to work. Therefore, the helping professions tried to help people by *addressing their symptoms*. This was done by working with a patient's negative past or negative feelings, or by trying to change negative behavior. These approaches were difficult and stressful for the helpers *and* for the people being helped. It was hard to accomplish lasting change or make too much progress. It was as if helping professionals were bailing out a leaky boat while the water was still rushing in through holes in the hull. Without knowing how or where to fix the boat itself, to make it strong and seaworthy, bailing water is always a losing battle. What has been missing is the recognition, at a deeper level, of how people carry their past with them through time.

Findings About the Source of Self-sufficiency

People carry the past into the present using the vehicle of thought. They carry ideas or expectations based on how they have *innocently interpreted* their past. One of the first things Dr. Mills and his colleagues found in their initial research on self-sufficiency was that they had been working in the wrong area with people. They were attempting to fix things at the "product" side of the chain of cause and effect. They were trying to solve problems often two or three steps after the source of the problem, or at least two steps down the line from where the suffering that was causing people's chronic unhappiness or dependency began. They were in the same situation as the farmer who locks the barn door after the horses have been stolen—they were already too late.

The authors found that the source of people's problems was not anything that had happened to them, nor was it their circumstances or their environment. Initially, it was hard to look beyond these factors. It seemed that all these things contributed to who people become as adults. Someone who learned to think that relationships define their self-worth will, at that level of thought, always be concerned about their relationships. Someone who learned to think they need lots of money to be happy will never have enough money. Someone who bases his or her self-esteem on their culture will always be suspicious or prejudiced toward people of other cultures.

Thought: The Missing Link

A closer look reveals how the link between things that happened in the past and how people live their lives today is always a thought. The link that had been missed was how people held these experiences in their everyday thinking, without realizing that they were viewing life through the ghosts of their memories. A memory is a thought—an illusion brought to life by the Principles. Wisdom and common sense allow us to see through this ghostly image, to live a happier life in the present free from any residue from the past. The authors started to realize that their clients had the capacity to see that the past exists only in memory. They could see the wisdom of not letting past thoughts control their lives in the present.

The source of every psychological problem is that people have learned to think about themselves and their lives in a way that causes them to *lose sight of their true potential*. Once their natural potential for common sense and learning was blocked by insecure thoughts, their lives started getting more and more difficult. For example, when a person is looking at something that happened to him or her through the filters of insecure thoughts, they think they are doomed. If they get laid off from a job, it means they are a failure. If their child is having trouble in school, they are a bad parent. If their spouse or friends are unhappy, they feel guilty.

On the other hand, all of these things look very different from a place of wisdom. Now if they are laid off, they will see the cause in less personal terms. If it is a sign that the business is doing worse, they may feel fortunate that they can go on to explore other opportunities. If their superior did have something against them, they may see that they could do things differently the next time to minimize the chance of being laid off again. Their wisdom has allowed them to learn from that experience. Or, if they do not buy into the thinking that they are a failure, they may use their unemployment time to get more training in areas that make them more employable or that are closer to what they really want to do with their careers.

As people free themselves from the grip of the past, they all demonstrate an incredible capacity for insight and for wise, healthy functioning. Psychology's focus on what is wrong and its well-meaning efforts at trying to alleviate the symptoms of suffering and dysfunction have caused some helping professionals to miss people's innate resources for health, for learning, and for natural motivation. Everyone's potential for satisfying, productive, responsible lives has been underestimated. People's ability to understand how they work mentally and cure themselves by allowing their resiliency—their "undamageable" health and wisdom—to emerge has also been underestimated.

Just the Facts, Please

Surprisingly, it is easier to share the three Principles with people than to try to *change* their thinking, their emotional reactions or their behavior. Knowing what Thought is—and what it does to determine how things look to us—automatically brings us back into alignment with our wisdom.

People can then see how they have *unwittingly brought their past into the present* via their thinking. They can also see an alternative to making their thinking from the past look just as meaningful now. They can recognize and appreciate the value of their healthy, responsive and more objective thinking. They see that engaging this natural healthy thinking is the source of their resiliency.

The next chapter will explore the finding that understanding the Principles is, in itself, enough to start resiliency and sustain change. A common question about Principle-based healing is, "What can I do to access this natural wisdom?" The answer is that there is nothing to do, except to increasingly see the Principles in action more clearly and to be open to deeper feelings. Chapter Eight will address this vexing "how to" question and explore how we can continue to access more beauty and understanding in the course of living life everyday.

How Understanding and Deeper Feelings Lead To Change

Chapters Four and Seven explored how insecurity, in the form of unrecognized "conditioned" thoughts from the past, can interfere with realizing true potential. Because the past now exists only as learned habits of thought, we can free ourselves from the past by learning how to access our healthy thinking. This chapter explores our ability as human beings to change from the "inside out." This change is not merely a trade of one belief system for another. It is a genuine shift in understanding that frees us from the past and from learned and habitual ways of thinking. Principle-based programs in clinics, organizations and communities showed that shifts in thinking can free our children, and us, from habits carried across generations.

An earlier passage in this book discussed findings from different forms of therapy and counseling that demonstrate how people's outlook seems to change in sudden bursts of insight. These kinds of insights do not take us deeper into our insecure thoughts—they show us how to bypass them. Following each insight, there is a certain amount of change, which then levels off until we have another insight. It is always insight that produces lasting change in behavior. No one can change his or her behavior until perspective shifts. Once that occurs, new behavior looks normal and obvious rather than unattainable or difficult.

The dilemma is that we cannot force or program an insight. We can only stay open to the experience and realize how Thought is both the conduit and the barrier to insight. If we accept the thought, for example, that life can't change because of a horrific past or current hardships, that very thought will keep us mired in the past or in the problem.

A shift in perspective is not, in and of itself, the magic wand that lifts people out of adverse conditions of poverty, hopelessness or lack of education. It can, however, give them the wherewithal and motivation to access their inner resources and start to change these conditions, both for themselves and their children. It gives people an understanding that, collectively, they can change their lives, families, communities and organizations.

The Limits of Changing Others

It is impossible to force or manipulate people into changing their thinking patterns. Accessing our healthy thinking is something we can only do for ourselves. The success of marketing strategies may make it seem as though people are highly suggestible. But the best marketing firms study what consumers are *already* thinking and what they feel they need. Advertisers market products to respond to shared beliefs. People are most suggestible when they are wedded to thoughts that make up their self-image and/or drive desires. This understanding points people to a more profound recognition of Thought, at a level from which they see the Principles at work before they form any self-concept or self-image. When people realize that thoughts create their desires and their need to be accepted, they find a less conditional kind of self-esteem. Understanding Thought at this profound level is something people can only do for themselves. People change more easily when they see how their learned *habits of thinking* have made them prisoners of the outside influences that affect their behavior.

Most of us have had the experience of changing our minds. The process is not a mystery. We change our minds about what we want to eat for supper. We change our thinking about our favorite songs or colors or sports teams. These changes appear effortless because we understand these particular thoughts are completely under our control. In other words, we know on some level that the choice is ours to make.

Understanding Thought at a Deeper Level

There are, however, thoughts that have a different feel. Sometimes our thinking is so automatically conditioned that it appears as if we have no choice but to think what we are thinking. Our thoughts seem to be controlling us, instead of the other way around. By understanding the Principles, we can regain control over our thought processes.

A client shared a story about how understanding Thought helped shed new light on a situation. Whenever she accompanied her husband on a business trip or to a business dinner, this client agonized over whether she would be able to hold up her end of the conversation, or if she would be thought of as interesting or witty. She always harbored these anxious thoughts to the point of feeling a big knot in her stomach. She assumed it was the circumstances of meeting new people that produced the knot in her stomach, so she would often plead a headache and beg off joining her husband on business endeavors. This created stress in their relationship and additional personal stress for the woman.

Once this woman began to understand the role of her thinking in creating her experience, she felt great relief and the knot in her stomach lessened. She began to relax and enjoy the business outings with her husband. As she relaxed, her innate health and humor emerged—and not only did her husband enjoy and appreciate her company more, but so did his clients.

Increasing our personal understanding of the Principles, the role of Thought and our potential for deeper feelings are the primary avenues for lasting change.

The authors' work over the years has led to the discovery of several basic pointers or clues that are evident in everyday life. These pointers can assist people in raising their level of understanding about the Principles to help them understand their thinking at a very practical level. These pointers or clues are: 1) the role of positive feelings; 2) putting the past in perspective; 3) recognizing moods; 4) using feelings as signals; and 5) accepting separate realities. Chapter Nine will explore each of these pointers in greater detail.

These pointers should be regarded as just that—clues or tips on how to stay pointed in the right direction. However, it is important to clearly reinforce the finding that change becomes natural and effortless when we see that *the real point is simply to raise our levels of consciousness.* Chapter One defined Consciousness as the ability to both experience reality and to recognize the source of experience. Every time we see the Principles illuminating an uncharted area or working to a deeper degree in our lives, we have raised our levels of consciousness and attained a *new level of understanding.* Higher levels of Consciousness merely reflect an increased level of understanding about how reality is created.

Levels of Understanding

Deeper positive feelings are the catalyst for people to change their minds. Raising our understanding of Thought floods us with desirable feelings. The connection between understanding the Principles and accessing our deeper feelings is a powerful one.

Rather than trying to figure out our thinking or analyzing our progress, the best lubricant for getting us unstuck and releasing us from our habits of thinking is allowing ourselves to experience deeper feelings. When we look for a feeling that is not connected to our judgments about outside events or not connected to proving our self-concept, we immediately open up to more understanding. We want to point ourselves to a feeling of tranquillity, well-being and security that comes from inside, not outside. This feeling is free—it is not dependent on changing anything. This feeling flowers into insights that shed light on how we use our thinking and on how Thought works to create a personal world, self-image and range of feelings.

For example, a drug addict or alcoholic who wants to change may feel guilty or ashamed about what he has done in the past, both to himself and to friends or loved ones. These bad feelings are tied to outside behaviors. The problem is that these feelings lower his spirits and cause even lower moods, spiraling downward to shame or self-hate. These times are when he may feel like he needs to get high or drink to escape from these negative, discouraged states of mind. These are opposite to the kinds of feelings that unleash common sense and wisdom, where change is natural and effortless.

Principle-based projects with drug and alcohol treatment centers attempt to help people see their own innocence, to understand that they really did the best they could, given how overwhelming, hopeless or frightening their lives seemed to them at the time. When they realize that they were doing all they could to escape the hell created from their learned habits of thinking, they forgive themselves and find more rewarding feelings. When they are treated by staff and the people around them as healthy and capable of making better decisions from their healthier thinking, they start to feel better and drop attachment to their insecure habits.

Many of these people were able to quit using drugs or alcohol *on their own* once their natural, less conditional good feelings came back and their common sense clicked into place. As their insecure thinking started to look less real, the urge to use drugs and alcohol dropped accordingly. They were then able to understand and resist the urges that stemmed from the physical aspects of addiction, or they felt motivated and hopeful enough to get into detox and move back into their everyday lives at a much healthier level of functioning.

Unconditional deeper feelings were both the trigger for and the source of immunity, as these people realized that positive feelings were better and much less costly than the high they got from drugs or alcohol. These deeper feelings were also much more productive than those they obtained from comparing themselves or judging how they were doing by society's standards or looking for the approval of others.

Understanding the Principles or raising levels of consciousness helps people see where their *experience of life* begins. If they can see that their experience starts with Thought and expands from there, they are looking in the right direction. It is powerful to see our thinking unfolding from inside—to see the movement of Thought as it transforms into feelings and behavior. When we reognize this flow, life becomes understandable. Change results naturally and effortlessly from deepening our ability to see how Thought *works*. The best way to approach learning about Thought is without blame or judgment for others or ourselves.

When we slow down our habitual thinking,
we allow the mind to work the way it is
meant to work.

The Hard Road to Change

Any time someone tries to make a change through guilt or shame or "shoulds," he or she is actually just making change harder. If change doesn't seem obvious or matter of fact, it becomes difficult to accomplish. If change is not interesting and fun, it will not last. Through "forced" change, people see the world one way and try to behave another way. Usually what people do is feel frustrated or guilty, generating bad feelings that lower the quality of their thinking ("I can't do it," "I'm not good enough," "I should know better").

When people feel bad and are not thinking clearly, they slip back into their old habits.

One deeper feeling that contributes greatly to change is gratitude. It is a paradox that change is more difficult when we are dissatisfied. If we are genuinely grateful for whatever we have in our lives and don't feel the need for anything to change, we open ourselves up to change. *Gratitude is a feeling that fosters insight.* It gives us more peace of mind, which opens the door to wisdom. A sense of humor—the ability to laugh at ourselves and our foibles, as well as to not take life too seriously—is also helpful. If we experience these kinds of feelings more of the time, our wisdom will start to emerge to help us in life.

The Easy Route to Change

Change is fun, easy and simple when we use common sense, see things clearly and use our innate wisdom. When we function in a healthy way, new ideas flow naturally to us about how to do things, about what we want to do and enjoy doing, and about what seems helpful and manageable. We don't have to *try* to change our minds, emotions or behavior. All we have to know is how the Principles work and what Thought does and how it manifests differently, depending on our thinking in the moment. All we do is quiet our thinking and let our healthy thought process take over.

When we realize how change works as a natural process we look for feelings that aren't conditional; deeper, calmer feelings that aren't tied to the behavior of our kids, our jobs, our grades or our friends. We keep an open mind. We are receptive to new ideas and intrigued by the idea of looking at life in different ways. In simple terms, having an open mind and enjoying life are all it takes to keep us growing and changing in positive ways.

The more we realize about Thought, the more we realize that healthy, liberating changes keep happening—almost in spite of us. *We don't need to analyze or figure out our thinking.* We don't need to be serious or anxious about change. We don't need to worry about what anybody else thinks. We don't need people to give us advice, plans or techniques for change. We have simply realized a fundamental fact about where our experiences of life come from—*inside us.* Levels of understanding signify how deeply a person realizes or sees this fact about the link between Thought and life.

Deeper, positive feelings are important and helpful in raising our levels of understanding. People should not be encouraged to increase or bring out negative emotions as a route to change. This way to change is bumpy, like constructing barriers on a racetrack to make driving harder. Positive feelings "grease the wheels" of positive change.

Chapter Nine will review the logic of this understanding and distill our observations of how people gain this understanding into some practical guidelines or tips on how to stay pointed in the right direction toward deeper wisdom. However, these tips are *not* intended to become techniques or rituals. When ideas become ritualized, the pointer tends to become the destination. The thing that we worship or honor becomes the ritual, taking precedence over the real goal or destination toward which that hint or clue is pointing. All anyone can do is provide clues—things to notice and recognize as pointing toward the deeper operation of the three Principles.

CHAPTER NINE

Staying Pointed in the Right Direction

This chapter will look at how positive feelings help us gain perspective, leading to better outcomes in any situation in life. It will explore how this kind of positivity is different from trying to make ourselves "think positive." It will look at putting the past in perspective so that whatever happened in the past becomes less stressful or limiting in our present lives. It will look at how moods work in daily life, and how they provide opportunities to teach us about our thinking and our innate mental health. Finally, it will explore how understanding Thought and separate realities can assist us to more clearly see the Principles in action.

The Role of Positive Feelings

The term "positive feelings" does not refer to pumping ourselves up or forcing ourselves to look at something in a more upbeat way. The term merely refers to the ability to relax for a few minutes, put our worries aside and simply enjoy ourselves. If we can even temporarily let go of our cares and not dwell on things that upset us, our natural good feelings return. What we really want to do is to appreciate and savor those times when we are not self-conscious, when we aren't thinking about ourselves or about anything worrisome or serious. If we can see this ability as something very helpful, the experiences that are enjoyable, relaxing or carefree will multiply. They will become more frequent and last longer.

Learn to see the value of allowing yourself the time to relax. Empty your heads and become immersed in something that takes your minds off of yourself. The authors had a client who was the vice-president of a large corporation. He had worked his way up from driving a truck and supervising line workers. Many of the other VPs had business degrees from Harvard and seemed to be much more prepared for this level of management, both intellectually and in their real world training. The client became insecure about being in over his head and got into drugs to quiet his insecure thinking and keep himself going. By the time he came in for therapy, he had a $500-a-day cocaine habit. He had lost his wife and his home, which created more guilt, shame and insecure thinking.

Once this man learned that he could transcend his self-defeating habits of thought, he started to realize that his real value at his current level of management was his wealth of experience. He realized that he could bring a unique perspective on what the line level workers needed and on how they experienced their jobs. He settled down and stopped using drugs. He said that whenever his insecure thinking started up again, he would notice it before it took over and take a short walk to clear his head. Or he might just ask his secretary to hold his calls and turn on some music he loved. He would stop work and just get into enjoying the music for a half hour or so. His healthy state of mind returned when he distracted himself from his insecure thoughts and relaxed, with nothing else on his mind.

When people are in a positive frame of mind, they have more common sense. They are less apt to dwell on their past. Higher-order feelings contribute to a spontaneous upward shift in levels of understanding. In other words, a positive perspective contributes to mental health.

All this may not be new to you. It makes sense that *life looks better when we feel better*. Unfortunately, people often feel badly because of their circumstances—or think they should. Many people are suspicious of good feelings. Many people believe that if they get too happy or relaxed, everything will fall apart. What people need to realize that they can *do* better once they *feel* better—and they *can* feel better, regardless of circumstances.

Like the chicken and the egg, people feel badly because of what they have done—or what has been done to them—up to now. From this perspective, it is hard to see ways to do better. Yet most people believe they can't *feel* better until they *do* better. Once people feel better, this alone helps them understand the relationship of their feelings to the quality of their thinking.

Positive Feelings in Action

A client from a public housing intervention program told the authors she was afraid to feel too good because then, "everything would start to go to hell in a hand-basket." She felt she had to constantly stay vigilant and ready to fight. She and her children slept on the floor at night because she was afraid of stray bullets from gang wars over drug money.

When this woman first came to parenting classes, she would often fall asleep. This happened partly because of how tired she was, but also because the feeling in the class was safe, secure and relaxed. Her mind finally slowed enough to let her fall asleep. Although she missed some lessons, the effect of her exposure to warm, deeper feelings was evident and positive.

She soon heard enough in class to realize that her insecurity and fear came from habits of thought. She started to question some of her insecure thinking. She found more relaxed feelings. These feelings helped raise her level of understanding and she recognized she had something wise and true within her that would help with her children and her situation. These insights strengthened her feelings of hope and changed her outlook. She transferred to a larger apartment out of the way of gun battles. She saw more productive ways of handling her children and they started to do much better in school. As she began to improve her own life, she became an active force in organizing other residents to make the entire community better.

Helping Ourselves in the Worst Circumstances

The authors once met a parent whose older sons were dealing crack and other drugs out of her apartment. Her two daughters were on crack and prostituting themselves to support their drug habits. Her youngest son and daughter were seldom in school and were more comfortable hanging out on the street with their older brother's friends.

The mother felt ashamed and embarrassed, overwhelmed and hopeless. She had dropped out of school herself, was living on welfare in public housing and felt she was a failure. Other residents who had been through Principle-based parenting and leadership courses encouraged her to attend the classes. At first she sat quietly in the back of the room, too ashamed to talk. She listened to other people talk about similar problems and learned that she was not as different as she thought.

As she began to feel better, she realized she possessed her own self-esteem and common sense. She took charge of her family. She saw that she could show her children love and at the same time be more assertive and helpful in steering them toward better lives. One of her sons is now out of the drug trade and has a job. The other has moved out on his own. Her older daughters are both off the streets, off crack and back in school. Her younger children followed suit.

Positive feelings emerging from within people who have learned about the three Principles have brought about extraordinary change in even the most "dysfunctional" families. Once a person's health is uncovered, it guides that person to solve her own problems in the ways she sees fit.

People don't change because they are wrong.
People change because they discover their health.

Putting the Past in Perspective

Understanding the role of the past is another important contributor to mental well-being. While a person may have been exposed to a great deal of negativity in the past, the only way anyone can carry the past into the present is *through thinking*. Although a bad experience is real at the time it occurs, we suffer from it in the present only when we hold onto it in our everyday thinking.

A person may have been put down, abused or subjected to prejudice and neglect while growing up. While these experiences are tragic and children should not have to go through these kinds of hardship and traumas, *the actual damage carried through time is not from the experience itself*. Two people can join the army and go through basic training. In boot camp, both are yelled at, told they are the scum of the earth and made to go through grueling physical punishment. One person can think: "This is the army's job as my officers see it. It doesn't make sense to take it personally. Let me just get through it the best I can, without making too much of it."

Another person may think the drill sergeant doesn't like him because he is worthless, and this recruit may take on the feeling of worthlessness. He may feel abused and resent the physical and emotional punishment. Whenever that person remembers his experience of boot camp, it will lower his spirits and make him feel bad about himself.

The real difference between the two people is that one took the experience to heart in his thinking about himself. The first person realized that boot camp was something he had to go through and it said nothing about him as a worthwhile person.

Research on resiliency shows the same patterns for children. Past damage is only carried across time when a child takes the experience to heart in her thinking and continues to process self-destructive thoughts. Past damage is always reversible. Past trauma can be cleared away by simply realizing that it is only old thoughts held in memory. Moving away from this past-related thought brings people back into their health in the here and now.

Once we learn to stop making too much significance of memory, we automatically start to heal faster from past negative experiences. Dwelling on a negative memory interferes with the natural healthy functioning of our common sense, which is more interested in the possibilities of the present.

> *Living in the present allows us to use our capacity*
> *for common sense, objectivity and insight*
> *more of the time.*

For all human beings, seeing life new and fresh has important advantages and can help make their lives better. Resiliency research shows that most people eventually get over their bad experiences. The process accelerates when we realize negative thoughts about the past can be dropped without fear, promoting higher-order feelings in the present and healthier functioning throughout our lives.

This process is "jump started" when we trust that there are good feelings available to us right now. Just trusting this fact will help. We then know that it is a good idea to take our minds off our problems, to look for humor and a lighthearted stance toward our problems. We will find that good feelings will start to sneak up on us, taking us by surprise. These feelings will bring clarity, insights and new ideas.

When we are burdened by problems, it often seems as if we should stay intensely focused on them, stay worried and serious. Yet it is only by being willing to admit you do not know what to do—and trust that something new will come to us—that we can have fresh ideas that will help resolve our problems.

The Role of Moods in Daily Life

Everyone has good moods and everyone has bad moods. Moods reflect the amount of insecure thinking in our heads at any given time. Moods are fluctuations in our levels of mental health. Our mood levels determine the degree to which we feel compulsively attached to things on the outside in order to find well-being or self-worth.

When we are in a good mood we see things in a more positive way. We show more patience. We are more enthusiastic about life. We appreciate others and we experience more enjoyment. In our good moods, we tend to bring out the best in ourselves and others. We are at a higher level of mental health.

In a bad mood, everything is opposite. We overreact; we are more defensive and paranoid. We take things personally. We think our friends don't appreciate us. We resent our partners and our children. We feel hostile, depressed and apathetic. We feel we have lost our mental health.

Low moods are insecure states of mind. The presence of insecurity means our minds generate a lot of thoughts that make us self-conscious, anxious or full of self-doubt. In an insecure state of mind, we feel less control. We feel more at the mercy of outside occurrences. Our well-being seems dependent on outside sources of gratification. People feel the urge to drink and use drugs to "cope" when they feel insecure.

Other urges, like overeating, spending money and showing off, are compelling when we are in insecure states of mind. Parents may feel compelled to yell at or put down their children. A person might get angry with his friends and pick a fight, or go out and drive his car too fast, while another person might brood or even feel like killing himself. These behaviors are all the consequence of low moods and insecure states of mind.

One of the most helpful things to know is how to recognize and navigate low moods. *Negative thinking generates low moods*. Low moods generate more negative thinking and the downward spiral continues, ever more severe. The way out of this vicious cycle is to recognize that we are caught up in a lower level of consciousness. When we realize that our negative feelings of despair or guilt are just *thoughts*, we are suddenly not as gripped. Low moods pass—usually on their own—if we don't feed them with more low-mood thinking.

Recognizing Feelings as Our Guidance System

Although moods have a huge effect on our perceptions, with an understanding of the Principles we are able to recognize them. Our feelings provide feedback on our thinking and let us know about our moods. Physical pain, for example, is the body's way of telling us that something is wrong. Without pain, you could touch a hot stove and do serious damage before realizing you needed to remove your hand.

Negative feelings such as hostility, self-righteousness, selfpity, envy or depression signal us that our moods have dropped and our thinking has become distorted.

When we have these kinds of feelings, our thinking is not guiding us well. In those moments our thinking is our own worst enemy. It is time to stop whatever we are doing, step back, take a breath and relax. We must resist the impulse to struggle, fight or judge. If we wait patiently, wisdom will eventually shine through like the sun after a rainstorm and we will find the answers we have been looking for.

*As people increase their understanding
of how thoughts produce feelings,
they realize that the positive or negative quality
of their feelings is a guide to how they are
functioning psychologically.*

Thought and Separate Realities

Human beings have all learned to think differently. No two people see things the same way. Even best friends do not see everything the same way. These differences make life interesting but, without understanding, can also be the source of conflict between people. A point of view or way of looking at life is neither right nor wrong—it just is. When we don't know how thought works, our outlook is based on past experiences and conditioning. It is *how we learned to think about things*.

When the authors first launched Principle-based projects in public housing, they found a lot of mistrust and hostility between neighbors. There was a great deal of fighting and physical violence. Teenagers would shoot one another over a girlfriend. Gang members would attack people they didn't know just because those people were wearing another gang's colors.

Leadership classes taught residents how everyone has learned to look at things in different ways. The instructors talked about how learned ways of seeing the world can appear to be very real. The classes explored how these learned ways of seeing lead to disagreements, fights and feuds.

Violence and conflict began to subside as residents recognized that everyone sees things differently and that everyone is innocently stuck in his or her particular version of reality. People became less suspicious of their neighbors simply by entertaining the idea of separate realities.

As they let their guards down, neighbors became friends. They went from not allowing their children to play with one another to sharing babysitting duties and throwing birthday parties for each other's children. They pooled resources such as money, furniture, food and clothing. One council put on a fundraiser for a neighboring migrant community that had suffered tremendously as the result of a winter freeze. Another council hosted a Thanksgiving dinner for the homeless population in the surrounding community. They fed more than 100 people. Residents recognized that by putting aside their separate realities they could work together to solve common problems.

Another example of the value of understanding separate realities takes place in a corporate setting. A top exective from a health care organization related this story to the authors: The senior management team was required to cut a million dollars from the overall budget. In the past, before the team had gone through Principle-based training and understood separate realities, they had gone away for a two-day budgeting retreat to figure out how to reduce the budget. The budget would be cut—but only after much competition and negativity over the weekend.

This time the team met and, within one hour, successfully strategized on how each division could cut its budget to achieve the needed reduction of one million dollars. The executive who related this story said there was a deep feeling of rapport and alignment during this meeting and many creative ideas occurred to the team. She mentioned that cutting the budget meant that the team members understood that there was a chance one of them might lose their job, but still the team worked together for the greater benefit of the organization, understanding that if they were living in integrity, another opportunity would take its place.

Because of their understanding of the Principles, this management team had much more respect and appreciation for one another's points of view and for the unique needs of each of the separate departments. Rather than making their own needs paramount, the team members wanted the result to be fair and equitable and to maximize the benefit to the entire organization. The following chapter will explore in more depth the way that relationships, across the board, are affected when the people in these relationships understand how Thought makes up each of their realities. They can then appreciate how and why each person's thinking looks real to them, and they can know how to use wisdom to make their relationships better. With understanding, all relationships can continue to improve and grow in the level of mutual enjoyment, satisfaction and discovery over the years.

CHAPTER TEN

Building Healthy, Rewarding Relationships

When people begin to realize their own health and wisdom, they automatically do better in all their relationships. One of the first things they recognize is that it is their own thinking about a relationship that helps it improve or deteriorate. While we cannot be responsible for how others see us, we can choose to either see their health or allow ourselves to get caught up in judging and reacting to their behavior. The more deeply we touch our own health, the more easily we see through people's learned ways of coping. Once we realize they are doing what makes sense to them, we see their psychological innocence. Once we recognize that somehow their feelings of well-being or security look threatened, we won't take their behavior personally. We can then see the health underneath their habits of coping and responding to others.

This is not to suggest that others should not be held accountable or responsible for their behavior. But it is also true that we cannot be responsible for other people's behavior or for their thinking in a relationship. We can only take responsibility for our own thinking and behavior. No one could reasonably suggest that you should stay in a rocky relationship, particularly if it is abusive. Yet if we can see our relationships with clear eyes, without the filters of the past, we often see ways to make it better. The first thing that will change is that we will be much less tempted to take the other person's behavior personally, whatever they are doing.

It's Never Personal

When you start to function with more wisdom—and with less contamination from your own past—you will see that you have innocently picked up a lot of ideas about how you need to act or cope to feel secure and prove your self-image. You will see others innocently doing the same thing. You are less tempted to take things personally because you recognize that their behavior is not directed at you. People don't usually act with malicious intent, although it appears that way when we take things personally. They act from within the thought-created "cocoon" of their own reality. They act to defend their own reality, to feel safe or to protect their self-image. They do what they *think they need to do* to survive or feel good about themselves.

A woman in a community program became unemployed and had to apply for food stamps to feed her children. The food stamp worker was someone with a lot of prejudice toward people in that situation—she felt they were all lazy and liked being dependent. Her self-image rested on being a hard worker and pushing herself to do more. She treated her clients rudely and made them wait around and jump through unnecessary hoops to get their food stamp applications approved. While others reacted angrily, and some even stomped out without completing the application process, the woman from the community program felt compassion for the food stamp worker. She could see that this poor soul was not enjoying her work, that she was angry, impatient, stressed and unhappy every day at work because of how she viewed the people she was serving. The client, because of her level of understanding, did not take the worker's attitude or behavior personally.

Because of her understanding of thought and separate realities, this woman realized that the food stamp worker's behavior was not personal. The food stamp worker was reacting to her own thinking. The client also realized that this person was likely so stressed and upset by the end of the day that she took her bad mood home with her and probably took it out on her spouse and children. In fact, because this applicant was not rattled but was compassionate and patient, she had a smoother time getting her application processed.

Another client had a husband who suddenly started getting home from work later and later. She could tell from his breath and behavior that he was stopping in bars and having a few drinks. When this behavior got worse, she began to think he didn't love her and had to get drunk to handle coming home. When she came in for help, she started to understand what was going on. Her husband was feeling insecure about his job in a company that was downsizing. As he took on more stress at work, he became more anxious and agitated. He feared he might lose his job, and not be a good provider. At this point he felt that he needed a "pit stop" on the way home to calm himself down and deaden his insecure thinking about work and his role as a provider.

When the woman realized that her husband's behavior wasn't personal, but merely his way of coping with his own insecure thoughts, she could stay on his side and help him feel more secure and better about his work situation. By being compassionate and understanding, she helped him realize that he could come home and let go of his insecure thoughts there. Then he wanted to come home rather than feel compelled to stop and have a drink.

Separate Realities and Common Sense

When we live more deeply in our health, we take everything less personally. That does not mean that we put ourselves in harm's way. We also know to use our common sense to get out of the way of physical danger. One of the reasons that physical abuse and family violence were reduced so rapidly in many of the Principle-based community programs is that people started using their common sense in situations that could easily have escalated. People were able to see that their self-worth came from inside, from their own natural states of well-being and self-esteem. It did not come from the other person, or from the quality of their relationship, or from how their partner or children were treating them. Because they were less reactive, they did not do as many things that pushed the other person's buttons. They could see that making the other person feel judged or acting in ways that triggered their insecure thinking was counterproductive. They were also more aware of when the other person in the relationship was getting insecure and upset. They could then take steps to either de-escalate things or get themselves out the way of any harm.

On the other hand, if it appeared that one partner was unwilling to change, then the other, using their common sense, sometimes would leave and move on with their life. The authors have seen many couples in this situation get back together again with far more love and respect for each other.

Some of the youth in the Principle-based community groups who had a history of abuse became wiser and more aware of the danger signals and learned to seek shelter at a safe haven. And if the authors saw a child in danger, they would get the child out of harm's way as quickly as possible, at the same time working with the parents to help them understand their thinking of the situation. Once the parents had stabilized, the authors would talk with the caseworker and assist the parents and children to reunite.

The fascinating thing was that when people saw their relationships less in terms as who was right or who was wrong—less from a stance of blame or judgment, either toward themselves or the other person—they took much better care of themselves. Blaming the other person, or feeling guilty or at fault ourselves, keeps us hooked into relationships in an unhealthy way. This is partly because our thinking isn't as clear in these feeling states, and because we want to justify or defend our own behavior or make the other person see where they were wrong, or make them pay for what they did, or try to "get them back."

When we see the fact of separate realities and how real people's insecure thoughts look to them, we can make any relationship move toward becoming a much healthier one, for ourselves at the very least.

Rapport and Deep Listening Dissolve Separate Realities

As mentioned in Chapter Nine, everyone sees things differently. Furthermore, we also each have thoughts that are important to us that are not as important to others. One couple told the authors this story of how the two of them had very different ideas about how their home should look and feel. The wife felt at home, relaxed and cozy when her son's toys were strewn around the house, when she had shopping bags and clothes draped on the furniture and around the living room. Her husband was fastidious and tidy. To him, her idea of a "comfortable and cozy" home looked like a pigsty. This difference was always a source of conflict and upset until they both dropped notions about who was right and who was wrong and re-established rapport. Then they could start to respect each other's separate realities and work out a reasonable, mutually satisfactory solution without either one making the other "wrong."

Traditional models of couples or relationship therapy emphasize being honest about our feelings, being "up front" and standing up for ourselves. The problem with these models is that when we are upset, we do not see things clearly. Remember that our feelings start with our thoughts. When we are estranged from our own wisdom, our insecure habitual thoughts connected to our self-image are the thoughts that seem most real and important. When we express anger or upsets, we usually do not see the bigger picture. We do not see how the situation looks to the other person with whom we are involved. These models tend to drive people further apart rather than closer together. When the other person is feeling attacked and blamed, he or she is more likely to retreat into insecurity and fear, and to defend their reality. Both become attached to their separate realities and move away from their wisdom and compassion.

The worst time to attempt to discuss or resolve issues in any relationship is when you are upset. The wisest thing you can do at this time is to step back, calm down, and re-establish rapport. You will then be able to listen and grasp how the other person's behavior makes sense to them. With deep listening, you will be able to help the other person move out of insecurity to engage their healthier thinking. When both are able to address and resolve issues or conflicts in this healthier state, you will find that the solutions are more creative and certainly wiser and more satisfying than the ideas or solutions that occur when we are imprisoned in our separate, conditioned habits of thinking.

People with whom you have relationships will appreciate the fact that you can stay calmer when they are upset. Your ability to refrain from retaliating on a personal level will help them look at what they are doing and give them a chance to see their own thinking and feelings with more objectivity. Most of the things that people make "right" or "wrong" in relationships are connected to their past and to their learned ways of thinking. If we can clear our lenses, by realizing this fact, we won't make the other person wrong for seeing things differently, but will be curious and interested in how these things look to them.

Many people are suspicious of the value of not taking things personally because they feel they have to defend themselves or risk becoming a doormat. There is actually a third option, which is to stay in our wisdom while seeing that the other person is merely defending the way that reality looks to him. This perspective keeps us from becoming insecure and feeling compelled to defend or maintain our self-concept, as well as providing an opportunity for the other person to re-engage their wisdom.

By staying open, interested and nonjudgmental, we are more likely to help others look more objectively at their own thinking about relationships. They may be able to gain some distance from the things that bother them and "push their buttons," and this distance will enable them to see their issues differently. When we make others "wrong," we usually bring out the worst in them. When anyone is feeling pushed or threatened, they are more likely to become defensive and frightened, more likely to lash out and defend their beliefs. When they are feeling respected and safe, they can stay in a good mood and are more likely to see their thinking as more arbitrary. They may start to see their expectations and "shoulds" as less important than maintaining a good feeling in the relationship.

A woman in a Principle-based professional development course was a school psychologist. She was dedicated to helping youth have more self-esteem, to enjoy learning and become more self-motivated in school. She had a conflict-based relationship with one of the more senior faculty members at her school. Early on in their relationship, this man had resisted some of her ideas for bringing self-esteem programs into the school. He felt that learning the "three Rs" was most important. He believed that discipline and structure allowed the teacher to stay in control of the class. Staying on task while not "molly-coddling" the students was more important than the "feel good" stuff she advocated. As she hardened her stereotype of him, it became standard that they would get into heated, sometimes acrimonious, arguments at faculty meetings. Both of their positions hardened over time to the point that they would automatically resist each other's proposals or ideas without really hearing one another out.

The woman attended a training session held for her school district and started to see how people can get locked into their positions. She started to see the psychological innocence of her combative colleague. She realized that he had been at this school a long time and was dedicated to the reputation of the school and to the idea that students should learn in his classroom. She could see that he had some legitimate concerns, and realized that he had never felt listened to in his relationship with her.

The next time the psychologist wanted to propose a student program related to self-esteem, she took it to this man first. She shared some studies with him on the relationship between self-esteem and learning, and she asked for his advice about how to introduce such a program without taking valuable class time away from academics or threatening the ability of the teacher to maintain control in the classroom. She told him that she recognized his legitimate concerns and listened more openly to what his concerns were. She then modified her proposal to address some of these concerns. To her surprise, and to the astonishment of everyone else on the faculty, he supported her proposal for a self-esteem program at the next faculty meeting.

Listening Deeply with an Open Mind

Relationships are much more rewarding and engaging if we can listen deeply, beyond our own thinking about another person and beyond any judgments or conclusions about what they are doing. Even people we have known for years, including parents and partners, can show new facets of their personality or interests if we are open and curious. However, we often make up our minds about who they are and what they have to offer, and we think we know them. It is easy to fall into the rut of our own thinking about people we have known for a long time. We even expect them to respond in certain ways to specific issues, situations or problems. Sometimes we do this to such an extreme that we are defensive or blaming before they even open their mouths. When we are adamant and defensive, we will, more likely than not, get what we expect—an argument from the other person defending their reality.

When we stay open and interested, we give the other person the best opportunity to grow and tap into their healthy thinking more deeply. A friend of the authors recently ran into such a situation. She liked to shop and saw it as her "job" in the family. Her husband was more interested in sports or being on his boat during his free time. She got very busy in her job just before a planned trip to see their children, and was distressed because she felt that they would not be able to bring any presents for their granddaughter. One night she came home and found that her husband had stopped at a toy store and purchased perfect presents, surprising her by demonstrating that he knew what their grandchild's favorite toys were. Their granddaughter loved teddy bears and had quite a collection. The child was going through a difficult time and was having some trouble sleeping. The grandfather had found a book for children her age about a bear that was having trouble sleeping. This woman had been married more than 30 years, and yet her husband's behavior surprised and delighted her. It broke her stereotype of who he was.

Everyone has the innate capacity to grow and broaden their horizons. If we live more deeply in our healthy functioning, we will continue to grow and learn everyday. If both people in a relationship move into healthy functioning, living more in wisdom, they will grow together and learn from each other. From this vantage point of curiosity and an open mind, relationships will continue to change and deepen, becoming richer and more rewarding.

Rapport: Seeing and Engaging Health

Seeing the health in others, while looking past their faults or insecure habits, acts as a catalyst to bring health to the surface more of the time. Having a stake in seeing someone else change is not a way of recognizing their health but rather a means of focusing on their learned habits of coping. When in a healthy state of mind, these habits either do not catch our attention—or they even seem endearing. We can see their innocence and the struggle the other person is having. When we are in a more insecure frame of mind, these habits are annoying and we are more likely to take such behavior personally.

When we focus on health, people will surprise us with how they grow and what they can do. When we do not make judgments or jump to conclusions, it takes the limitations off their ability to have new insights, to change and grow. The authors have a friend whose wife was musically inclined when she was younger. She had taken piano lessons and played the flute and trombone in the high school band. When she studied nursing in college she felt that she did not have time for music. Then she married and had children, seeing herself only as a wife and mother. As her children grew, she wondered how she could stay fulfilled and contribute to the people around her.

This woman thought her music days were behind her. She started to feel bored and sometimes even depressed when her children did not need her as much. Her husband had the insight that he was also seeing and treating her only as a wife and mother. He recalled her talking about her interest in music as a teen. He encouraged her to take up the piano again and join a local group that needed a piano player. When she decided it might be fun to get back into music, she was amazed at how well she did and how much the group appreciated her talent. She began a whole new life, and the husband willingly took over some of the household chores so that she had the time to pursue music.

While not everyone will start a whole new hobby or career, it is possible for everyone to find a more rewarding, deeper appreciation for life and for engaging in their interests more fully and with more enjoyment. In fact, given the way the mind is designed to work, with wisdom and insight as our guide, this will happen naturally when people live more deeply in their health. All that is required is that we do not limit our thinking, about either our own potential or the potential that others bring to the table. Seeing health is one of the most beautiful things we can do for people in all our relationships.

The Power of Forgiveness

Forgiveness is one of the most powerful tools to keep our relationships close, satisfying and enjoyable. Many couples, for example, hold onto resentments—about real or imagined slights or hurts—for years. When people we love do things that cause us unhappiness, that hurt our feelings or that don't meet our expectations, we start to build up layers of thinking about all these past events. Some couples hold onto everything the other person has *ever* done to them, to the point where they are annoyed and ready to pick a fight as soon as their partner walks into the room. Sometimes they don't listen at all, because they think they already know what the other person is going to say and they may even hear what they expect to hear—even when the person in is a different state of mind and doesn't react predictably. When they are upset enough they can go through the entire litany of resentments. All this habit does is to keep the quality of the relationship at low ebb. Then it normally takes something special or unusual to bring back the romance and caring that got them together in the first place.

True forgiveness comes from the wisdom of seeing that whatever anyone has "done to us" was the best that person could do at the time, given what their thinking was like, given what looked real to them and what seemed threatening to them. Because everyone is innately healthy, they will not intentionally do anything to hurt us unless they are themselves feeling attacked or misunderstood.

The Power of Our Own Health and Wisdom

Once people have gained understanding for themselves, they are often eager to share it with the people who are important to them. Sometimes they are too eager. We cannot really explain our own insights or realizations to others. Even if people are open and eager, they are seldom able to see beyond their own thoughts, their own judgments and their history in a relationship. When we are too eager to share something we have found for ourselves, it can be taken as feeling superior and may only trigger defensiveness or resistance.

The best way to share understanding is to live it, by being graceful and accepting and by showing more patience. If we take things less personally and maintain good feelings, others will notice a difference in us.

If we listen better to hear how things look to them, they will be grateful. If we see common situations in a wiser way and come up with better solutions and decisions, people will notice. Sometimes, just by osmosis, other people will start to slip into their wisdom and health.

Seeing others we care about as people who are innocently living life the best they can is powerful. We are freed from the burden of our negative feelings or reactions to their behavior. Forgiveness helps the forgiver first and foremost. Again, this kind of forgiveness doesn't mean that we should put ourselves in harm's way. It just means that we are not dragged into the feelings of resentment, jealousy or anger that the other person may be experiencing. We can then see how to get out of the path of danger and still be effective in making the relationship better over the long run.

Many of the women with whom the authors have worked in family violence programs were able to first get out of harm's way by moving out—staying with a friend or at a shelter, or moving back in with their parents, aunts or other family members. They changed locks, got restraining orders and did what was necessary, because they felt capable of functioning on their own and used common sense. They were able to respond to their partners with understanding in a way that helped their partners to recognize their own insecure thinking. Their partners could then seek help to eliminate the grip their negative thinking had on them.

One woman who came to a three-day program struggled with the idea of innate health. She could see the possibility of health in children and a few other people but not in her ex-husband. She had experienced domestic violence in her marriage and harbored a great deal of anger and bitterness toward her exhusband. Whenever her ex called to arrange to see the children, she would be curt and rude and would angrily give the phone to one of the children. This created further resentment between her and the children.

When she left after the first day of the program, she continued to mull over the idea of health living naturally within everyone. She had an insight that this was true, and when her ex-husband called that evening, she was in a calm state and feeling joy at her discovery of health. She spoke to him in a warmer manner and they had a better conversation than they had had in a year. He was curious about the change in her and ended up apologizing for his poor treatment of her.

When she came to the training session the next day, she was bubbling over with enthusiasm. She was amazed at what had transpired in their conversation. This gave her more faith to continue to see health in others.

Three years later, she was married to a wonderful man and had a good relationship with her ex-husband—and *great* relationships with her children. This understanding changed her life, helping her to not only understand her ex better, but also her father, who had abused her as a child. She saw how her habitual thinking had kept her anger and bitterness alive and left her unable to see any possibility of change in her ex-husband or father. Now, with new understanding of the role of Thought and innate health, she has been able to let go the past and start a new life. She is now a well-respected trainer specializing in domestic violence issues.

No one wants to do harm to someone they love. In a variety of family violence programs with which the authors have been involved over the last 10 years, staff consistently report that the perpetrators feel ashamed, guilty and confused about why events got out of control. When the participants in these programs began to understand the Principles, they recognized the role of Thought in creating their moods. They got control of their behavior because they knew it was fueled by their thinking. They became respectful, loving and responsive, even those with a long history of abuse. They too were able to walk into a new world.

When we walk into the world of health and wisdom, everything changes. Relationships will change over time, if we can maintain our bearings and treasure our new-found feelings enough to not let personal history or a stake in a relationship pull us down. When we find higher ground, we want to show others how to get there, primarily by example, rather than jumping back into the quagmire of problems caused by taking things personally because of blame or ego.

Learning to be selfless in close relationships is one of the hardest things we can do. Yet it is a constant opportunity to confront our beliefs, our egos and the minefields of our own personal thoughts. If we can trace our discomfort and hostility back to our own thinking rather than taking these feelings out on others, we always learn more about the deeper dimension of thought. We will find many of our relationships turning into beautiful, harmonious partnerships, sharing deep feelings of gratitude, love and satisfaction.

The concluding chapter will extend the logic of this understanding one step further to explore how these discoveries can have an impact on society as a whole, including relationships between countries and cultures. More and more of the professionals and institutions with an understanding of the three Principles are beginning to recognize the global implications. They see the possibilities for accomplishing exciting positive steps in cross-cultural understanding, in peacemaking and in learning to respect every ethnic group, religion and society across the globe—even among groups whose hatred and prejudice goes back for generations.

CHAPTER ELEVEN

The Benefits for Society of Understanding These Principles

The discovery of the Principles that form moment-to-moment reality seemed miraculous to the authors at the beginning of this journey some 25 years ago. The idea that everyone has a deeper wisdom available to them at all times seemed far-fetched. This revelation flew in the face of everything the authors had learned, both from our life experiences and from the way that the field of psychology has developed since Freud. Yet this discovery imparted a tremendous sense of hope and fresh optimism. As Principle-based programs evolved and the truth of this discovery became more apparent, it was easier to point people past their habits of thinking to this deeper intelligence and to help them find a wisdom that gave them understanding about their lives. After 25 years of working in the fields of community mental health, community revitalization and corporate leadership, the authors have seen people at all levels, living in every kind of circumstance, unleash deep wisdom as they recognized these Principles in action.

Contrary to what many "experts" said about their past or current situations, people in the most dire straits, who were overwhelmed by their daily lives and full of hostility and fear, were able to directly access a deep and healing inner wisdom. After recognizing even a glimmer of the Principles of Mind, Consciousness and Thought, people changed without working on themselves, struggling with their problems or analyzing past traumas. Thousands of people have found an understanding that made happiness available immediately. These positive feelings opened the door to insight, which led to finding more wisdom. People began having insights about how to live more satisfying and meaningful lives. These changes made them even happier and more productive.

Residents of disadvantaged, crime-ridden communities, as described in Chapter Six, and now documented in many other studies, directed this wisdom toward solving not only their personal problems, but also the social, economic, environmental and educational concerns in their communities. They got government agencies, school boards and the private sector to respond to their initiatives because of the quality of their insights, their certainty and dedication. Corporate leaders used their newfound wisdom to work smarter rather than harder, to reduce stress in themselves and their firms, and to discover increased creativity and innovation at all levels of the organization.

For all of these diverse groups of people, accessing clearer thinking brought with it newfound caring, compassion, patience and forgiveness. People saw the innocence of others, saw them suffering in the trap of their own hellish thoughts, and approached them from an entirely different perspective. When the residents of public housing reconnected to their wisdom, they saw the police much differently. While they disliked the way the police sometimes stormed in or bullied people in the community, they also realized that the officers had some compelling reasoning and conditioning that fueled this behavior. The residents were able to feel more understanding and compassionate and less judgmental when they recognized what the police felt that they were up against. They then shared insights with the police about crime prevention and how to reduce crime rates.

The authors have observed similar, very powerful changes in perceptions between ethnic groups who had been bitter enemies, and even in rival gang turf in crime-ridden communities. The authors have observed corrections officers in jails, probation officers, teachers in alternative schools and staff in programs for delinquent youth change their viewpoints entirely and treat their wards with genuine compassion and respect. All of these people started to recognize their own psychological innocence more deeply, engage their own health, and provide hope in a way that opened up the possibility of entirely new lives for those with whom they worked.

Because of these experiences with communities all over the country, the authors do not hesitate to say that wisdom has been the missing link to healing society's ills. Even a minor increase in the level of wisdom of humanity would produce a new breed of more enlightened citizens. These citizens would possess the perspective and creativity to assist policy makers, intellectuals, corporate leaders and government find innovative, compassionate and more positive approaches that can effect genuine, fundamental, even revolutionary progress in the workings of society. In a true democracy, citizens engage in healthy dialogues rather than attacking one another from disparate camps. Such an increase in wisdom would lead to strengthening this kind of relationship between citizens and their representatives within any political system.

Wisdom and Society

Society is currently beset with ethnic prejudice, civil discord and centuries-old hatreds. Wisdom produces understanding, the solvent that cuts through these *thought-created* barriers. It is the capacity that allows people to see through the "separate" illusions that create societal prejudice, fear, rigid beliefs and judgments and to recognize our common humanity. When people regain their wisdom, as a community or culture, the see that they don't have to live in fear or dominate and control others. Until people look at others with wisdom, violence and manipulation may look necessary for their survival. Hate or hostility seem justified. Irrespective of the form of economic or political system we put in place, these systems are run by people who themselves learned to think in ways that tend to perpetuate fear, control and competition. A recent article in *The New York Times* described a long-running war that had culminated in attempts at ethnic cleansing by both sides at different times (depending on who was winning the civil war at the time). This war began with a burst of hatred that started during a conflict more than 800 years ago. Few of the citizens of these two ethnic groups in this country even know when that war happened or what caused it. The hate became so ingrained in their collective thinking that it has fed on itself for successive generations. Their leaders felt that they had to keep fueling this hate to stay in power.

While there is fear and insecurity in the world, there will be inequitable political and economic systems. While we may wish to build more egalitarian systems, people will always find ways around them. As long as these myopic qualities of thought look real and meaningful, there will be a lack of vision for the long-term sustainability of our environment, and sometimes a short-sighted focus on profit, competition and the immediate gratification of consumerism and "winning." As long as humanity focuses on and is frightened by our surface differences of race, income, religion or ethnicity, conflict will remain the status quo. Some societies will hoard a surplus, while others will starve. Ethnic cleansing and retribution will continue. These conditions are kept in place by thoughts that look real and compelling to people, even though they are "made up" and almost invariably result in prejudice and inequity.

Societal Realities and a Universal Intelligence

When people recognize the existence of wisdom, they take their personal thoughts less seriously. From then on, their thinking automatically discerns the purer, spiritual intelligence that exists before form. It really is that simple. Insecure thought, learned and acquired from outside, from our environments, from our cultures, and from exposure to others people's beliefs, is merely a smokescreen. It can be quickly cleared by understanding. Insecure thoughts can be learned from the frameworks of widely disparate social or political beliefs. Yet, as Einstein succinctly put it, "God doesn't roll dice." When we look inside ourselves, we realize that there is a deeper intelligence in life, in nature and in the inner spirit or energy behind life. It permeates life; it provides the life force that turns energy into form and vice versa. This intelligence acts to bring life into harmony with itself. It doesn't take a doctorate in psychology, physics or any other science to have a deep understanding of life. Such an understanding comes with simply seeing how Mind, Consciousness and Thought create reality from the inside out.

Mental illness, hostility and insecurity exist not because of how we are put together, biochemically or genetically, but from generations of thinking, from ingrained fears, attitudes and beliefs in individuals, cultures and societies. Yet these seemingly insurmountable barriers to happiness are built completely from thought. Having more people exposed to the facts about how Mind works to create the myriad ways human beings experience life around the globe would in itself have a tremendous impact on the world. When we start to have experiences of deeper feelings of love and forgiveness, we may not even know why or how this change is happening. Suffice to say, people have insights, via their own wisdom, about the connection between forgiveness, love and their own mental health, as well as insights about the mystery behind life that is the essence of spirituality and the source of wisdom.

Contributing to Societal Harmony

Several years ago, a colleague visited the authors and became fascinated with their work. She admitted that much of what she observed did make a lot of sense to her, even though she had been taught that people need to go back into the past, acknowledge their faults and confront their negative feelings. Yet when she went back to her practice, it looked to her that she was being unreasonably harsh with clients and sometimes even contributing to their feelings of hopelessness about getting better. She found that she was now more inclined to give people the hope that they could leave a traumatic past behind rather than challenging them to re-engage in the feelings that came from their past.

When people malign those from other cultures and when governments attempt to control their citizens through fear, they are doing the same thing. They are holding on to injustices or resentments from the past. This stance perpetuates the underlying dynamics that contribute to holding onto the past with hate, bigotry and repression. When people begin to discover the impersonal, deeper wisdom already within them, they see the harm that prejudice and hatred do to the world. They cannot imagine why those thoughts made sense or seemed meaningful and real to them before.

After observing the inspiring results or programs based on this understanding at a community level, it is easy to recognize that taking these discoveries to a societal level could have a potentially wonderful effect on us all. We could spend several lifetimes attacking issues of poverty, drugs, crime, education, prejudice and environmental issues community by community—but if we could help to accelerate a shift toward realizing this enhanced wisdom, it would trigger a significant rise in the level of consciousness of society as a whole. With this shift in consciousness, things would start to change more rapidly on their own, much in the same way that the Berlin Wall came down, suddenly, naturally and without a conscious campaign when the idea of the wall didn't make sense to enough people anymore.

The Link Between Personal Mental Health and a Healthy Society

The current levels of stress, pressure and craziness under which people try to function in our driven and competitive world not only affect their personal mental health but affect the quality of life of our society as a whole. Multiple studies have quantified the costs of the perceived pressures of the "rat race" and the spillover from greed and insecurity in society. They are astronomical. Self-help books addressing these sources of suffering become bestsellers. We cannot eliminate these qualities of thought by force or blame. Getting to our state of wisdom allows us to see, with forgiveness, how we made these points of view appear so compelling. What society would gain from functioning with increased wisdom would move us from a state of fear and toward a state of grace. A few years ago Roger met an African-American man who had been on death row for more than 30 years, mistakenly convicted of killing a white policeman in the South. Rather than succumb to a state of depression or anger, he kept studying the law and finding ways to appeal his sentence.

In 1995, with the help of a daughter who had participated in a community empowerment project based on the three Principles, he won his appeal, was pardoned and released. He appeared on *20/20*, *Good Morning America* and several news shows, explaining that he had never become bitter or hateful because he recognized the psychological innocence in his jailers and the trap of these feelings for himself. He came out of prison a joyful and inspiring human being, even grateful for what that experience had taught him.

When we understood how electricity worked, we were able to make our lives easier by harnessing that power. When we understand how the Principles of Mind, Consciousness and Thought work, and where wisdom originates, humanity can begin to access this beautiful resource. Wisdom can come to the surface in anyone at any time, without warning. Wherever it does surface, it addresses every realm of human problem. It helps people make more sense of their personal and professional lives as well as the balance between these worlds. As discussed in Chapter Ten, it helps people maintain better relationships. It helps people eliminate stress in such a way that they don't need to continually work on reducing the irritants that appear to come from outside.

As wisdom cleanses people's day to day thinking patterns, the decrease in stress in individuals and the corresponding rise in understanding across cultures and other groups in society will lead to a greater appreciation of diversity. The energy freed from hate and fear will lead to enhanced creativity and to new forms of culture, art and entertainment. It could also facilitate a deeper appreciation of nature and of the uniqueness that constitutes every individual. Some people might think that this kind of optimism is "pie in the sky" or even dangerous because it raises people's expectations about the possibility of a more utopian world. Some people have even stated that this view will make people naïve and more vulnerable to the evil forces of the world. However, the authors feel that no one is inherently evil, and that the feelings and behaviors that look that way are learned. We are taught to hate, to fear, to suspect and attack when we feel threatened. However, as Ghandi and Dr. Martin Luther King showed the world, we get a lot further with wisdom, compassion and love. Not only is such a change in the level of healthy, cooperative functioning possible in society, the route that goes through wisdom is the only way to get there in a sustained and lasting way.

Another criticism the authors have heard is that if society reached new levels of harmony, life would be boring. In fact, the exact opposite would be the case. With less stress and conflict, the extent of innovation and positive cultural and social change would approach the current level of freshness and creativity we are seeing with the rapid pace of technological change. Technological progress has accelerated at a dizzying rate. Information processing and instant access to data globally has increased a hundredfold in just the last five years. Yet our understanding of one another across the divide of cultural, religious and ethnic differences has not nearly kept pace. What has become repetitive and even boring is to continually repeat the same strife, conflict and wars over and over as a result of being "stuck" in old, familiar stereotypes, fears and hatreds.

More exciting realms of positive perceptual changes and societal advances would make things not only interesting, but would lead to newfound, deeper feelings now currently unfathomable. Such a shift would produce results such as the world has never before witnessed. Once a critical mass of people begin to realize their innate wisdom, watch out! Berlin Walls come down. Forced segregation ends. Colonial powers go home. Communities with high rates of crime become peaceful and thriving. Corporations become exciting learning communities with empowered employees. When wisdom begins to be unleashed at this broader level, we are in store for a more gratifying, rewarding and exhilarating life than we ever imagined possible.

Trusting the Unknown

For society to accomplish such a level of change, we need to be able to trust and explore the unknown in ourselves. We must be willing to drop our old beliefs and assumptions to look past surface appearances for a new logic or discoveries in science. As we look beyond the apparent forms that were visible to the naked eye in the physical universe, we realize that the forces and particles behind the physical are microscopic and invisible. When we look beneath the contents of our current habits of thought, beliefs, prejudices and conditioning, we see the fabric that produces reality before form. We discern the Principles of Mind, Consciousness and Thought. We then have the understanding and trust to quiet our minds, to relax the grip on our learned habits of thinking and realize new levels of wisdom.

Because we are just beginning to grasp these underlying Principles, the journey to deeper levels of wisdom, and to new possibilities for global harmony, is essentially never-ending. With all the good that the work of practitioners of this understanding have already accomplished, we are on the verge of a new consciousness that can take humanity to new vistas of societal change and creativity. Rather than fearing the unknown, we should be thrilled and fascinated by the possibilities that can appear by simply opening our minds, hearts and souls and relaxing into the quiet within that brings newfound wisdom, grace and discovery.

ABOUT THE AUTHORS

Dr. Roger Mills is one of the pioneers in the development, testing and application of the Principle-based paradigm in psychology. Dr. Mills received his undergraduate degree from Princeton University and a multi-disciplinary Ph.D. from the University of Michigan. Dr. Mills has taught at the University of Michigan, U.C. Berkeley, the University of Oregon, San Jose State, Florida International University, the California School of Professional Psychology and the University of Miami. His pilot-demonstration projects have been funded by the National Institute of Mental Health, the U.S. Department of Justice, The National Institute on Drug Abuse and major private foundations. Dr. Mills is the author of *Realizing Mental Health* (1995) and co-author (with Elsie Spittle) of *The Health Realization Primer— Empowering Individuals and Communities* (3rd edition, June 2000). He has published numerous professional journal articles and is an international consultant, speaker and trainer. Dr. Mills is currently Chair and Co-founder of the Health Realization Institute, Inc.

Elsie Spittle is an internationally recognized trainer and consultant. She was one of the first people to elucidate and teach the Principles upon which the Health Realization understanding is based. She is the co-author (with Roger Mills) of *The Health Realization Primer—Empowering Individuals and Communities*, and she is recognized by many practitioners as an expert in personal and professional development. Ms. Spittle currently heads her own firm, which specializes in coaching, mentoring and leadership development.

RESOURCES FOR FURTHER READING

Banks, Sydney. 1989. *Second Chance*. Tampa: Duval-Bibb Publishing Co.

Banks, Sydney. 1990. *In Quest of the Pearl*. Tampa: Duval-Bibb Publishing Co.

Banks, Sydney. 1998. *The Missing Link*. Edmonton: International Human Relations Consultants, Inc.

Banks, Sydney. 2001. *The Enlightened Gardener*. Edmonton: International Human Relations Consultants, Inc.

Mills, Roger and Elsie Spittle. 1998. *The Health Realization Primer—Empowering Individuals and Communities*. Long Beach: Health Realization Institute, Inc.